Praise for *Cultivating Curiosity*

Curiosity is the most important word in education today. Teachers the world over long for ways to cultivate this elusive yet essential path to engagement and authentic learning. After a dreadful year of heroic efforts to engage students in remote learning, *Cultivating Curiosity* offers a much-needed blueprint for the journey back to face-to-face, hands-on, problem-based teaching and learning. Over a brilliant, pathbreaking career, Doreen Nelson has developed and refined an innovative methodology that nourishes curiosity, stimulates creativity, and scaffolds critical thinking. This is the first important education book of the after-pandemic era that every teacher, every parent, every policy maker and concerned citizen alike should read with gusto and to much profit.

—Marcelo Orozco, Chancellor, University of Massachusetts Boston

In the end, Design-Based Learning is all about creating a vehicle for students to connect abstract academic concepts to concrete ideas, and to imagine creative solutions to challenges that they confront along the way. It provides a context for students to "perform" their thinking and discoveries. Ideas that they learn in one application may well turn out to serve another field or situation equally well. Hence the learning becomes integrated in an important way and, as opposed to a building of requirements, can serve as a frame of curricular design.

—Lorne Buchman, President, ArtCenter College of Design, Pasadena, California

I frequently look back with gratitude to my experience in Design-Based Learning-focused classrooms during my three years at Walnut High School. Now, I am studying to become a teacher with the hope to pass along the innovative education I am thankful to have received.

—Madeleine Skinner, alumna, Walnut (Calif.) High School

Since 1994, I have been championing the Design-Based Learning methodology in classrooms in Japan and in an exchange program we had with Finland. Doreen's methodology was a crucial part of guiding our students to come to terms with the devastating events of the earthquake that hit Japan in 2011. For five years, in cooperation with the Japan UNICEF Association, we used the Doreen Nelson Method of Design-Based Learning at the Sendai City Shichigo Elementary School as a comprehensive learning template for reconstruction. We have continued implementing the methodology thereafter, and more than 1,200 children have experienced its power. This book will significantly impact many of our teachers and their students.

> **—Dr. Shinya Sato, Professor, Yamagata University, Yamagata, Japan**

Doreen Nelson has put pen to paper to share her innovative instructional method of Design-Based Learning, in this brilliantly written and engaging book. Nelson has given us the gift of understanding how education can inspire students to learn and teachers to teach by igniting the curiosity in both. In the spirit of John Dewey and through a hands-on, contextualized approach, students taught using Design-Based Learning acquire knowledge across multiple subjects and develop higher-order thinking while being challenged to consider the milieu of society's most pressing issues and to develop strategies to address them with creativity and care. I can think of no more relevant or important methodology for teaching today.

> **—Christina (Tina) Christie, Wasserman Dean & Professor, UCLA School of Education & Information Studies**

. . .it has been astounding what you were able to accomplish in preparing so many students for creative thinking, I tell my granddaughter about how we were exposed to a variety of experiences that helped shape who I am. No doubt my experience in the 5th grade, having you as my teacher, has had a very long-lasting impact on my life.

—**Portia Stots, student in the first Design-Based Learning class**

I want to thank you for your innovative and creative use of the "City" in your methodology, because it turned me into an urban planner. . . . I became curious about how cities are designed, how decisions are made in cities; so much so that I obtained a master in urban planning (UC Irvine) and a doctorate in geography (USC). And now I teach at CSULB using cities as a framework for understanding policy development.

—**Rigo Rodriguez Ph.D., Board President, Santa Ana Unified School District; Associate Professor of Latina/o Public Policy, Department of Chicana/o and Latina/o Studies, California State University Long Beach**

Design-Based Learning started as a grassroots movement in the San Gabriel Unified School District and now has become one of the major initiatives for developing 21st Century Learning Skills in our students. We have seen students flourish in our Design-Based Learning classes, engaged with their learning and excited about creating and collaboratively solving problems. Our teachers have embraced the methodology and have found it to be a refreshing alternative for integrating the core curricular areas into a meaningful and exciting learning experience. We utilized the Design-Based Learning methodology as a district during the pandemic, collaborating as an organization to successfully create "Never-Before-Seen-Solutions" to problems new to us in public education. Design-Based Learning continues to expand in our district as the benefit of this type of authentic learning takes hold.

—**Jim Symonds, Superintendent, San Gabriel Valley Unified School District**

It's been such an honor and so exciting to be on this never-before-seen journey with Doreen and the Design-Based Learning family she has built. Now, with this book, her methodology can be shared more broadly with teachers, students and the entire educational system. *Cultivating Curiosity* will have enormous impact.

—**Jessica Heim, Director of the Design-Based Learning Project, Center X, UCLA**

Doreen Gehry Nelson's methodology has changed me fundamentally, and I cannot wait for more people to know about the Doreen Nelson Method of Design-Based Learning. Doreen is a true inspiration for so many, and her vision is what pushes me and others to become better educators.

—**Stephanie Na, AVID (Advancement Via Individual Determination), Advanced Composition, and Special Education English 2 teacher, Workman High School, City of Industry, California**

Doreen Gehry Nelson believed in us, and in doing so, she guided us through to a wonderful dream come true.

—**Angela Gurrola, Spanish teacher, Gabrielino High School, San Gabriel, California**

The Design-Based Learning Method has changed my life, and most of the lives of our children.

—**Natalie Bezdjian, kindergarten teacher, Rose & Alex Pilibos Armenian School, Montebello, California**

Doreen has been a true inspiration to me and to so many. She has shown us all how to persevere even when life sends us never-before-seen-challenges. Her words of encouragement and wisdom have stayed with me and now they serve to inspire many others.

—**Araceli Garcia, English Department Chair, Workman High School, City of Industry, California**

Congrats to Doreen on the realization of her dream. Design-Based Learning has been a source of inspiration and joy for me and for my classroom. I know this book will be a new beginning to share her vision with the world.

—Georgia Singleton, 4th grade teacher,
Roosevelt Elementary School,
San Gabriel, California

Doreen's method has revolutionized my way of teaching. It is the base of creativity and analytical thinking for future generations.

—Anna Cruz, 5th grade teacher, Roosevelt Elementary School,
San Gabriel, California

Many years of hard work are inside this book. And it inspires. In all seriousness, Doreen's Design-Based Learning method frees teachers. It has changed my view about the role of education for all who participate. And, it has opened my eyes to how fun, serious, and exciting education will find those that ask 'why.'

—Dave Cameron, science teacher, Gabrielino High School,
San Gabriel, California

The work of Doreen Gehry Nelson will bring innovation to classrooms for years to come. Thank you to being so devoted to raising our profession to the next level.

—Daphne Chase, 2nd grade teacher, Wilson Elementary School,
San Gabriel, California

Expanding on the work of John Dewey, Doreen Nelson has made the nuances of constructivist pedagogy concrete, relatable, and engaging. She provides a comprehensive guide that works as a catalyst for creativity, collective consciousness, and civics in any classroom. It is an antidote to prescriptive programs that unwittingly restrain and disengage students and teachers from higher-order thinking. *Cultivating Curiosity: Teaching and Learning Reimagined* offers hope to anyone interested in the connections between our fragile democracy and schooling. Educators at any grade level, parents and policy-makers alike, will find this design-based learning methodology a tool to integrate disciplines and reflect on governance structures in thoughtful and fun-filled ways.

—Georgia Ann Lazo, Ed.D, Principal,
UCLA Lab School, Los Angeles

cultivating
curiosity

cultivating curiosity

teaching and learning reimagined

DOREEN GEHRY NELSON

The Doreen Nelson Method of Design-Based Learning

JB JOSSEY-BASS™
A Wiley Brand

Jossey-Bass
A Wiley Imprint
111 River St, Hoboken, NJ 07030
www.josseybass.com

Jossey-Bass books and products are available through most bookstores. To contact Jossey-Bass directly, call our Customer Care Department within the U.S. at 800-956-7739, outside the U.S. at +1 317 572 3986, or fax +1 317 572 4002.

Wiley also publishes its books in a variety of electronic formats and by print-on-demand. Some material included with standard print versions of this book may not be included in e-books or in print-on-demand. If this book refers to media such as a CD or DVD that is not included in the version you purchased, you may download this material at http://booksupport.wiley.com. For more information about Wiley products, visit www.wiley.com.

Library of Congress Cataloging-in-Publication Data is Available:

ISBN 9781119824169 (hardback)
ISBN 9781119824183 (ePDF)
ISBN 9781119824176 (epub)

Cover Design: Wiley
Author Photo: Carl Bower | www.carlbower.com

SKY10028696_081321

Photo: Carl Bower.

DOREEN GEHRY NELSON is Professor Emerita of California State Polytechnic University, Pomona, School of Education and Integrative Studies; Adjunct Professor in the Cal Poly College of Environmental Design; was a Professor at ArtCenter College of Design in Pasadena, California, from 2002 to 2019; and in 2019, was named Founding Director of Design-Based Learning by the UCLA Graduate School of Education and Information Studies–Center X for the UCLA Design-Based Learning Project.

An award-winning, 50-year veteran educator and published author in the field of education, Nelson began developing her Design-Based Learning methodology (formerly called City Building Education) in the late 1960s to ignite creativity, promote high-level transfer of learning, and foster cross-curricular critical thinking skills among K–12 students using the spatial domain. She was named one of 30 top American innovators in education by the *New York Times* in 1991, and is the recipient of both the American Institute of Architecture's prestigious Lifetime Honorary Membership (the highest honor for a nonarchitect) and the California State University's statewide, 2006 Wang Award for Excellence in Education.

Nelson has served as lecturer, teacher, consultant, and scholar-in-residence for institutions as diverse as MIT, Harvard, Apple Inc., Stanford University, the New Jersey Institute of Technology, London's Royal College of Art, Japan's Sendai Science Museum, the American Bar Association, Walt Disney Imagineering, and the Smithsonian Institution. Nelson contributed to the original Maxis SimCity simulation and wrote teacher guides for the product. From 1994 through 2004, she led a Japan–USA Cultural and Educational Exchange program to develop Design-Based Learning as part of the Japanese national curriculum. The program included international video conferences and a satellite school in Finland.

Nelson has taught her methodology to thousands of educators worldwide—and to architects and lawyers, researchers, computer scientists, marine biologists, medical doctors, theater artists, musicians, and dancers.

Encompassing four decades of evaluative data, Nelson's research confirms that students experiencing her Design-Based Learning methodology develop creative and critical thinking skills, and score higher than average on standardized tests in language, reading, math, and other subjects. English Language Learners and students with learning disabilities, too, show measurable improvement. Students in these classrooms graduate and enter college in significant numbers.

Nelson established a two-year master's degree program for K–12 teachers at Cal Poly in 1995, with an emphasis in Design-Based Learning; and a one-year certificate program in 2010. Three graduates of the MA program received a Doreen Gehry Nelson Design-Based Learning Scholarship in Cal Poly's doctorate program in Educational Leadership.

ArtCenter College of Design in Pasadena, California, hosted the annual, five-day Design-Based Learning Summer Institute for K–12 Teachers from 2001 through 2019, providing scholarships for participants, many of whom went into the MA program at Cal Poly.

In Southern California, Nelson's Design-Based Learning methodology is practiced in individual public and private schools; it has been introduced at the UCLA Lab School and is featured in the San

Gabriel Unified School District as part of its mission, and in the Los Angeles Unified School District in South Gate. The Walnut Valley Unified School District constructed a building dedicated solely to the Nelson's Design-Based Learning program at Chaparral Middle School, and established an Academic Design Program for 10th–12th graders at Walnut High School, applying the methodology to an integrated Math, U.S. History, World History, and Language Arts curriculum.

The UCLA Library Special Collections houses Nelson's archive with an oral history, and featured her life and work in an exhibition in 2017, the first time an educator has been so honored.

In 2019, Center X at the UCLA Graduate School of Education & Information Studies established the UCLA Design-Based Learning Project, led by a full-time director holding a master's degree in Nelson's methodology. In 2020, a gift of $2 million was given by the Frank O. Gehry Foundation to endow the Doreen Gehry Nelson Director of Design-Based Learning position for UCLA Center X, now the permanent home of the Design-Based Learning Project.

Doreen Nelson has done us all a service by deepening our ideas about pedagogy. Her method of Design-Based Learning is not so much a formula for teaching, as it is an all-encompassing approach to how we as teachers can guide our students to think creatively and make sense of what we are trying to teach them.

Students can't reuse information they don't understand. It is indeed odd how little official attention has been paid to the actual process and significance of teaching creative thinking. This book will be an exception.

I do not wish to summarize what Doreen Nelson is telling us. She presents her point of view with clarity and grace. But it is a privilege to introduce the evolution of her ideas. Teachers will benefit from her account. Her book will be a wonderful example of consciousness-raising in our field.

JEROME BRUNER
Distinguished Professor Emeritus
New York University
December 2015

With admiration and appreciation, I dedicate this book to teachers who have taken my Design-Based Learning methodology and run with it, and to those teachers who will be inspired to do the same.

Lynne Heffley, my editor and teacher, and a highly-gifted writer, was at my side as I wrote this book, opening the door for me to find my voice and think of myself as a writer. She is one of the kindest, most patient people I know. Working with her on this book has been a life-changing experience.

CONTENTS

FOREWORD

I have watched in wonderment as my kid sister, Doreen Gehry Nelson, has explored the world of K–12 education.

She has worked in the California school system and beyond for years and, along the way, she discovered that opening the floodgates of curiosity leads to all sorts of educational benefits. She experimented over the years with various teaching models that she developed and became quite practiced in the search for a better way.

Doreen has always understood that sparking people's curiosity opens doors to beneficial thinking. Over the years, based on this guiding principle, she has developed her Design-Based Learning methodology, which has proven its value time and time again. It engages individuals with their own feelings and their own ideas as they pursue the inventive experiences that unfold in the classroom under Doreen's methodology.

She has guided teachers to ignite their own imagination, develop their own intuition, and harness their own humanity in order that they can cultivate the same in their students. The power to imagine is the path to a better and richer and more equitable society for all. This is the power of the Doreen Nelson Method of Design-Based Learning.

I have participated in some of those events and have been personally inspired by Doreen's vision and her work. She is building a network of hope for kids, helping teachers light the fire of curiosity and possibility in their students. She is providing light at the end of the tunnel. I'm very proud to endorse her work.

—FRANK GEHRY, ARCHITECT

FOREWORD

I first met Doreen Nelson in the early 1970s. She had made an appointment to tell me about what was then called City Building Education (now called the Doreen Nelson Method of Design-Based Learning). She asked for my support in introducing her methodology in the small elementary school district in north Los Angeles County where I was the new superintendent of schools. Like Ms. Nelson, my beliefs about teaching and learning were influenced by the teachings of John Dewey and the Progressive Education movement, and the education that my three children received at the University Elementary School at UCLA (now called the UCLA Lab School). I was pleased with the notion of bringing her work to my middle-class, blue-collar community, where I thought the children would benefit from a cross-curricular methodology rooted in the teaching of creative thinking skills.

I told Ms. Nelson that if one of my school principals and one or more teachers at that school were willing to try out her methodology, she would have my support. After listening to Ms. Nelson's presentation, one principal brought the methodology to her school where two teachers agreed to learn to apply it in their combined upper-grade classrooms. Although I didn't pay much attention to what was transpiring, I did visit the classroom several times. The principal and the teachers appeared to be satisfied with the response of the children.

When I accepted a superintendent position in a considerably larger school district several years later, Ms. Nelson contacted me about implementing Design-Based Learning in my new district. Two principals agreed to try the methodology in several classes. Satisfaction appeared to be high until I received a call from one of the principals.

She said, "We love the program, everything is wonderful, but get Doreen out of my hair." Like an overanxious mother, Ms. Nelson was much too intense as she worked to assure fidelity in her methodology's implementation. She later told me that the incident led her to better teach and support teachers.

Although I believed that Design-Based Learning had great potential for improving student learning outcomes, educators were under pressure to improve achievement test results and were loath to risk trying new pedagogies, especially those that were unfamiliar. Making changes in the way teachers teach, even in the most favorable conditions, is difficult. After all, the grammar of schooling has not changed significantly since the mid-nineteenth century. Doreen Nelson was not deterred—discouraged perhaps, from time to time, but never one to give up on her vision of finding a more effective way to teach creative and critical thinking skills that will last a lifetime.

After a 40-year career as a K–12 educator, 23 as a superintendent of four California school districts, I accepted a full-time position as an Adjunct Professor in the Graduate School of Education & Information Studies at the University of California, Los Angeles (UCLA). I kept in touch with Ms. Nelson. I watched how the presentation of her pedagogy, first introduced 50 years earlier, matured and how successful her approach to training teachers became. Doreen has taught her methodology to cadres of teacher leaders in a master's degree program at California Polytechnic University, Pomona, and in summer institutes at the ArtCenter College of Design in Pasadena. I am delighted that Design-Based Learning has been adopted as an instructional method by several school districts. I am especially pleased to have introduced her Design-Based Learning methodology to Center X, the teacher education program that I was part of at UCLA.

There is now an Endowed Design-Based Learning Directorship in Doreen's name at Center X, a position currently held by one of Doreen's former master's degree students.

I am now retired from my second career as an adjunct professor and I am confident that the responsibility for carrying on Doreen's lifetime work is in good hands at UCLA, where it will grow the Design-Based Learning pedagogy to benefit future generations of learners.

—EUGENE TUCKER, EdD

INTRODUCTION

As a rebellious teenager, I would have laughed if anyone had told me that I would one day become a teacher and a teacher of teachers—and that I would love it.

I wrote this book imagining new teachers and seasoned teachers, who, like me, still aspire to make a difference in society through education. Most of us want to do more than just deliver dry subject matter to students. We want to prepare them for problem seeking and problem-solving around questions that are essential to society. We want the subject matter that our students need to learn to be put into a contextual setting that ensures their long-term memory retention so that they are able to apply what they learn to a wide array of situations. We know that teaching critical and creative thinking is the best preparation for an unknown future.

As a classroom teacher, it seemed to take me forever to understand where to look for answers to how to make learning stick, and how to teach in a way that would bring who I am, and my deepest family values, into my classroom.

In the late 1950s, my tough-minded, well-read mother, born in 1904, had just completed her high school degree, attending night classes at my high school. She had graduated with honors and was planning to go to college. At age 16, I had just graduated with a C+ average, and I agreed with my high school counselor that college wasn't for me. My mother disagreed in no uncertain terms. My entrepreneurial, endlessly creative, curiosity-driven dad (my role model) wasn't buying it, either. He had only finished the 4th grade and wanted both of his children to be well educated. My brother Frank (who would become the noted architect Frank Gehry), almost nine years my senior, my only sibling and lifelong hero, was excelling in his studies of architecture at USC. He told me that I was capable of doing something like that. I felt I had no choice but to go when my mother enrolled us both at Los Angeles City College (me during the day, her at night).

We had moved to Los Angeles from Canada after my dad's heart attack at age 47. In Los Angeles, with my dad too ill to work, the burden of supporting the four of us was on my mother's shoulders. She would come home at the end of the day from her job as a clerk at the Broadway Department Store in Hollywood, we would make dinner together, and after she tended to my dad, she would sit down with me and together we wrote essays for our classes and articles for the school newspaper, and studied for the sociology class we were both taking. My grades soared. I liked the teachers, the students, and the social activities so much that I decided to apply to UCLA.

As a student at UCLA, I went back to playing the harp, something I had studied seriously in middle school (with a harp my dad bought by working the night shift at a liquor store). I played in the UCLA Symphony for four years, and off and on in the Los Angeles Doctors Symphony. I changed my major a half dozen times, starting with Education, switching to Music, Anthropology, back to Education, then Sociology, then Art.

My brother Frank, meanwhile, had graduated from the School of Architecture at USC and with my family just scraping by, I had to be able to support myself. A UCLA counselor told me that if I took a few more Education courses and did supervised teaching, I could get a teaching credential in just one year, so I signed up—after balking at first because my mother had so often urged me to get a teaching credential to "have something to fall back on when you get married." (Perhaps she was recalling that when I was in grade school, while my brother built model airplanes and made sketches of everything, I had corralled neighborhood kids who were having trouble in school, had them draw pictures that told a story, and taught them to read.)

My family's belief in the inherent value of creativity, perseverance, doing things for others, and community activism is the bedrock for my life's work. In Canada, where I grew up, my dad, who was an American citizen, was politically vocal. While I was at Fairfax High School in Los Angeles, my favorite teacher was accused of being a Communist because she was against the supposed temporary relocation of residents in Chavez Ravine near downtown Los Angeles, where a new public housing project was to be built. (The city of Los Angeles had bought up that property through the power of eminent domain. The residents lost their community when the housing project never happened and the land eventually went to Dodger Stadium.) I joined protests against the city with my brother, and after that, during election times, he would take me to underserved neighborhoods to register voters and promote candidates.

When I became a teacher, I wanted to realize my strongly held belief that to equalize society, acknowledge cultural differences, and to prepare students to participate in a world of serious societal, political, economic, and environmental challenges, all kids needed to be taught to become courageous, original thinkers, capable of working together to make and evaluate proposals for change.

After 10 years of classroom teaching, I went back to school for a master's degree. I began developing my John Dewey-, Benjamin Bloom-, Jerome Bruner-inspired Design-Based Learning methodology. I zeroed in on two of the things that Bruner described as central to becoming an educated person: (1) creative thinking, the ability to imagine solutions to what would later be termed Essential Questions—the underlying powerful ideas, universal concepts, principles, values, and morals associated with high-level thinking—and (2) the ability to gather information from multiple areas of the curriculum to revise and refine what is imagined.

(I met Jerry Bruner in New York in the early 1980s when I looked up his name in the phone book and had the chutzpah to call him. To my surprise, he answered. After I explained that I had developed my methodology based in part on what he had written, he invited me to lunch. Jerry became a friend and supporter of my work, and I was honored and deeply touched by his offer [at age 100] to write the introduction to this book, in progress at the time.)

I eventually understood that during all my years of teaching, I had not been cultivating original thinking. I had long believed that building physical artifacts and role-playing within a contextual, cross-curricular "story" were vital for learning to become reusable. (Maybe it was my dad's passion for seeing how one thing could become something else that influenced me. As the owner of a furniture factory in Canada, he would explore how unique materials could transform the everyday products he designed and produced.) What I was missing was a way to unleash creative thinking in my students. That wasn't happening when the artifacts they made replicated what already existed and their "dramatic play" using those artifacts simply imitated others.

I wrestled with the meaning of Bloom's *Taxonomy* that pointed to creative thinking as the highest goal of education. Convinced that creative thinking is innate in all students, disenfranchised and privileged alike, and could be taught without sacrificing academic rigor, I began conceiving what would become the Doreen Nelson Method of Design-Based Learning (formerly called City Building Education) to put creative thinking skills first.

I had been successful at teaching the drill and practice of basic facts for Specific Transfer of Learning (2 plus 2 equals 4; 2 apples plus 2 oranges equals 4 pieces of fruit). I needed to find a systematic way to teach for Non-Specific Transfer of Learning that would open the door to creative thinking and enable students at any grade level to use and reuse information, think independently, and advocate for themselves and others. Accomplishing this, I thought, would build community and cultivate equality.

To discourage students from engaging in replicative thinking, I wondered what would happen if I had them "back in" to learning what I was required to teach them. After trying out numerous ideas in my classroom, I thought about how a city's character is reflected in its location, its architecture, and the values of the people who live and work there. I thought about how the parts of the city could be a metaphor for creative thinking and for all subject matter. What if I gave students a curriculum-based story about a city situated in a real place familiar to them, a story that asked them to imagine that city 100 years in the future? What if I had them build a rough model of their imagined City of the Future, shaped by their own Never-Before-Seen, roughly built solutions to subject-related, big topic dilemmas that they identified— *before* I taught them what others had done?

In the Doreen Nelson Method of Design-Based Learning, following its 6½ Steps of Backwards Thinking™, through a progression of big topic Design Challenges, students roughly build a tabletop City or other Never-Before-Seen built environments that represent real places or systems (a Never-Before-Seen Community, Settlement/ Colony, Ancient Civilization, Biome, Biosphere, Business, etc.), based on required curriculum.

Determined by a teacher's pre-set subject matter requirements and Guided Lessons, an ongoing City "story" evolves with students' original thinking displayed by the artifacts they build on individual land parcels to develop an ever-changing, dynamic model. Each big topic Design Challenge, taking place over a week to a month, integrates interdisciplinary studies and meets learning objectives in teacher-taught Guided Lessons related to big and small topics. Students bring their individual land parcels together—as parts to the contextual whole—in a continuing revision process as they review the problems they identify in their City and set out to solve as a classroom community the validity of their solutions. Social responsibility, social justice, civics, and government (division of labor and classroom management) come into play as students adopt government roles in the City through Never-Before-Seen Creatures they build as their Avatars.

The words "design" and "Never-Before-Seen" in the methodology are synonyms for creativity. A designer communicates original ideas, taking into consideration a client's "don't wants and needs" to make them real. In the same way, a teacher pretends to be the client, "hiring" students to be the designers of Never-Before-Seen solutions to Design Challenges, and requiring that they adhere to a "don't wants and needs" Criteria List.

This is not a competition to see who makes the best or prettiest artifact. Materials used for building can be anything, even folded cardboard or crumpled pieces of paper. There are no "wrong" answers *as long as students can justify how their Never-Before-Seen built artifacts meet the teacher's criteria. What the artifacts look like doesn't matter.* The tangible artifacts that students build, before revising them after Guided Lessons and textbook study, represent their original thinking about subject matter and promote the creative and higher level thinking skills that lead to the transferable application of information across the curriculum and in real life.

As students describe how their built objects meet subject-matter-related criteria, they learn to advocate for their ideas and to discuss and evaluate their solutions and those of their peers. Writing follows oral discussion. Students write about their creations and do required textbook study and related research. They use the information they acquire to revise their own built artifacts through oral and written presentations and/or by physically rebuilding them in the context of their

City's simulated government. This process, ongoing over a semester or school year, engages students in learning and gives them confidence and the vocabulary to think deeply about how the factual information they are required to learn applies to real life.

Design-Based Learning re-imagines classroom practice. It is not about stand-alone projects, arts-and-crafts activities, or training future professional designers. Creative thinking is woven into the entire K-12 required curriculum through this methodology, connecting multiple subjects to the student-built student-run City of the Future or other contextual environment.

Teaching at Cal Poly Pomona, California, gave me a university platform for training K–12 teachers through comprehensive course work in my methodology. To establish a Master of Arts Degree in Curriculum and Instruction with an emphasis on Design-Based Learning, I had to write a course of study and have it approved by the Academic Senate. This happened in 1995 with the crucial support and persistence of School of Education and Integrated Studies Interim Dean, Sheila McCoy.

To date, hundreds of teachers trained in the methodology have documented their practice and the significant standardized test results that their students have achieved.

In response to the Covid-19 pandemic, I spearheaded an online pilot program in 2020 working with a large group of K–12 Design-Based Learning teachers who were uncertain about how to apply the methodology online, but found that traditional teaching methods left their students disengaged. When technology first surfaced in the classroom, I had tried working with a few computer scientists to find a way to bring my Design-Based Learning methodology to a 2D medium without losing its fundamental reliance on the spatial domain: 3D, hands-on experiences. Those efforts were unsuccessful, but developing a pilot program with so many teachers anxious to apply Design-Based

Learning online made the difference. The results were that my methodology translated easily to the building and running of a City in a virtual setting, as long as students at home built physical artifacts for the City. What was learned from this online research will continue beyond the pandemic as a companion to in-person classroom teaching and teacher training. In a hybrid environment, my methodology will connect virtual and in-person teaching and learning by providing a continuum across both venues.

***

In the summer of 2019, I walked up the steps to Moore Hall at UCLA and entered the School of Education. My Design-Based Learning methodology had recently become part of the university's Center X teacher-training institution, one of the most prestigious in the country. I was there to oversee the first Center X Design-Based Learning teacher training.

I had gone up those same stairs on my very first day as a student at UCLA in 1955, intending to be a music major, not an education student, on my way to audition as a harpist for the UCLA Symphony. I couldn't help but choke up, thinking, "Oh, my God, I came here so many years ago to play the music of others. And now I'm coming to teach others to play the 'music' that I developed." It was a profound experience.

What I thought I would hate all those years ago had turned out to be a lifelong obsession, giving me the sense that I could make a difference in the world, something I've learned many teachers feel. When I was a classroom teacher, I often wondered why I was being paid to have so much fun.

Today, when I teach teachers, I feel the same way.

cultivating
curiosity

Creative Thinking by Design

Creativity is part of human nature.
It can only be untaught.

—AI WEI WEI

CHAPTER 1

NOT ARTS AND CRAFTS

Seven-year-old Amilie was inconsolable. She tearfully held up a smooshed piece of paper with one big, puffy, blue pom-pom attached. Her second pom-pom had fallen off and before she could pick it up, another student had stepped on it. To an outsider, the object in Amilie's hand might appear to be just a tangle of paper with a fuzzy ball dangling from it. But to Amilie, this was "Cottie," shaped by her own hands and imagination. And now Cottie was missing an eye.

Daphne Chase, her 2nd-grade teacher, asked Amilie how she might fix Cottie with the materials available, and Amilie gave it serious thought before deciding that two smaller pom-poms were the solution. "Now she's even better than before," she said.

This wasn't an arts-and-crafts project. It was the Design-Based Learning, Backwards Thinking™ process, reversing the standard teaching method to ignite creative thinking by having students imagine and build original artifacts as they develop and revise a tabletop City of the Future (or other curriculum-related environmental context) for a purpose: to activate Non-Specific Transfer of Learning so that students consciously use and reuse subject matter in multiple settings.

Thirty minutes was all it took for Amilie and Daphne's other students to complete building their Creatures/Avatars, the first of 10 sequential **BIG TOPIC** Design Challenges that Daphne would present to them monthly over the school year. Each Design Challenge was woven into a story based on the 2nd-grade curriculum and played out in the tabletop City her students were building. The "story" that Daphne told her students was that their City (built on a 30 × 60-inch table) was a magical place where their Never-Before-Seen Creatures/Avatars would be coming to live together as a community 100 years in the future.

Daphne's **BIG TOPIC** for her first Design Challenge was **LIVING THINGS**. To meet the state-mandated requirements for learning about animal life, and to prepare her 2nd graders to read about mammals, reptiles, and birds, Daphne had them create their Never-Before-Seen Creatures/Avatars out of found materials as they referred to her Criteria List naming the basic attributes of living things.

(The beauty of a Criteria List is that it, in a sense, becomes a surrogate for the teacher. When students say, "I don't know what to do," the teacher responds, "Check the Criteria List." Instead of asking, "Did I do it right?" students are taught to self-assess by using a Criteria List as their guide.)

Daphne asked her students to think like their Creatures, imagine what they ate, who the Creatures' friends and relatives were, where they slept, how they moved, what they were afraid of, what they dreamed of, their likes and their dislikes, and even when they would die! As the Creatures took on personal meaning for her students, Daphne referred to them to teach her **BIG TOPIC**–related, required Guided Lessons and to invest students in the evolution of the City they were building and would be revising.

Concurrently, Daphne introduced her students to ways to become a supportive community of learners. Over the course of a month, she taught them to give presentations about how and why their Creatures were Never-Before-Seen. They practiced being good listeners and how to politely question each other about how their Creatures were similar to, or different from, real animals they read about and why. The 2nd graders couldn't wait to explain how their Creatures' basic needs for survival compared and contrasted to those of all living things. They willingly listened to each other, read their textbooks, researched other sources that Daphne presented, and revised their Creatures according to new learning.

Before Daphne had assigned the Never-Before-Seen Creature/ Avatar Design Challenge, she asked her students to write about something important to them. Amilie wrote one page about Lego-land, "my favorite place in the whole world." A week later, Daphne had her students write about their Never-Before-Seen Creatures. Amilie wrote a seven-page, illustrated saga called "The Adventures of Cottie."

Daphne's Language Arts Guided Lessons taught her students how to augment their original Creature descriptions. Classroom disruptions were few as students met writing requirements, making booklets to showcase their work. In Science, they learned about the five senses as they categorized their Creatures' attributes. For Math, Daphne had the students measure each Creature and name the shapes found in them. Studying Civics, they role-played as their Creatures to learn how to get along and solve problems in the classroom. All of this prepared them for what they knew would come next: building a tabletop Never-Before-Seen City of the Future where their Creatures would live, work, and play.

This story grew over the entire school year, enthralling Daphne's students as she taught them to identify and solve a problem that she named as the **BIG TOPIC** for each Design Challenge. Her students learned basic subject matter through the required Guided Lessons—**small topics** supporting the **BIG TOPIC**—that Daphne taught across the curriculum.

Continuous assessments of students' ability to achieve the curricular requirements took place as the class experienced a new Design Challenge and multiple related Guided Lessons each month, taking place sequentially over the school year. For their second Design Challenge, derived from the **BIG TOPIC: PROTECTION**, Daphne's students built Never-Before-Seen Shelters for their Creatures on individual land pieces for their tabletop City. The students then built Never-Before-Seen Ways for their Creatures to move from place to place in the City **(BIG TOPIC: MOVEMENT)**, to get food and goods **(BIG TOPIC: EXCHANGE)**, and to have fair rules **(BIG TOPIC: GOVERNMENT)**. Integrated into the curriculum, each tactile, **BIG TOPIC** Design Challenge, followed by Daphne's required Guided Lessons, turned her students into captivated learners.

Daphne, a teacher in the San Gabriel Unified School District, is one of thousands of teachers worldwide trained in my Design-Based Learning, Backwards Thinking™ methodology. (The methodology has also been practiced for more than 30 years at what is now called the Open Magnet Charter School, in the Los Angeles Unified School District.) What happened in Daphne's class is typical of classrooms, virtual and physical, where teachers apply the methodology, whatever the grade level or subject.

BIG TOPIC Design Challenges propel a sequential "story" that evolves over an extended period of time within a student-imagined, student-built City of the Future or other reality-based, Never-Before-Seen environments rooted in required curriculum. Students take ownership of the "story" and its evolution as they learn to run their City of the Future, seek out **BIG TOPIC**–related dilemmas, and build Never-Before-Seen solutions to such questions as "What will living environments and social relationships be like in the future and why?" "What will a learning place be like and why?" "How will medicine be practiced?" "What can be done about pollution, overpopulation, and climate change? Mean people? War?" "What are the dreams, the hopes, the fears, and responsibilities of citizens, and how have people throughout history responded with unique designs when different cultures come together?"

"Design-Based Learning opens worlds of opportunities for learning that go far, far beyond the classroom and normal classroom skills," said Jeanne Miller, who teaches 7th- and 8th-grade honors-prep English Language Arts, Social Studies, Ancient Church History, and Family Life at St. Bonaventure, a Catholic school in Orange County, California. "Through the City my students build and my curriculum-related Design Challenges, I've had them respond to stories I make up about invasions, corruption, high taxes, unequal distribution of wealth, despotism, overthrows of government, and treason—Ancient Church

History provides a rich source of ideas! A creature is entrapped in a Never-Before Seen Jail Net high over our City at this very moment for attempted murder. But it's not all depravity and ruin. My Design-Based Learning practice has developed all types of interesting twists and tangents, with Design Challenges linked to TED Talks, and Guided Lessons about religion, lotteries, and stock markets. Design-Based Learning has facilitated any number of deep, mind-blowing discussions, with me absolutely dumbstruck at the wisdom, honesty, and courage of my students as they debate, discuss, and question and find their own answers."

By imagining and building their original solutions to dilemmas within a contextual, three-dimensional environment, students gain an invested interest in learning from textbooks and other research about how others have solved or approached the same dilemmas. Through this process, students learn that everything (objects, places, processes, philosophies, institutions) has been and will be designed by someone—and that *they* are a "someone," too.

Teachers immersed in applying the methodology say that a tactile buy-in to learning results in elevated scores on standardized tests, and fewer behavioral problems. They report that starting backwards—having students apply their thinking about subject matter to build Never-Before-Seen solutions to **BIG TOPIC** dilemmas before reading textbook examples, and having them compare their original designs to what they learn—triggers success.

"We do a Design Challenge before we learn what we have to learn," said Madeleine Skinner, as a 12th grader in the Academic Design Program at Walnut High School. (In August, 2020, Madeleine wrote, "It's been about six years since my first experience learning in a Design-Based-Learning-focused classroom, and now I am studying to become a teacher with the hope to pass along the innovative education I am thankful to have received.")

Promoting creative thinking to be accessible to everyone bumps up against the common misperception that originality is the singular domain of artists, scientists, mathematicians, and designers. My admiration for original thinkers has to do with their tenacity as they transform, rearrange, and translate information to make it their own, rather than replicating the work of others. It isn't surprising to me that students who are taught primarily to accumulate and replicate information about what others have achieved may relegate learning to a box labeled "school."

As a former classroom teacher, I know that there is something irresistible about telling students ways that they can do things better. If the **BIG TOPIC** is **SHELTER**, an elementary schoolteacher might want to say, "let me show you pictures of how bees make their houses, how a turtle carries its house with it, how Inuit people used to live on the ice. Could there be an igloo in the tabletop City you are building?" A high school History teacher might tell students about segregation and explain how it manifested unfair housing.

A Design-Based Learning teacher applying the method's Backwards Thinking™ process instructs students about real-life shelters for people or other creatures, for example, only after having them build their own Never-Before-Seen solutions for their City, referring them to a Criteria List derived from mandated subject matter standards and a set of conditions required for housing. After subsequent Guided Lessons, the teacher might say, "now that you have learned about how people through history have made their shelters in response to their environment and their needs, compare what you built to what you have learned and think of ways to revise your design."

The teacher still does what a teacher is supposed to do. What is different is that by having students first express their ideas about the **BIG TOPICS** and concepts they will be taught, the Design-Based Learning methodology sparks students' receptiveness to learning information from textbooks and other resources. Students are taught to apply what they learn in multiple ways as active, not passive, learners. They begin to think critically about how what they learn in the classroom has meaning for their lives now and in the future. (This happens when the methodology is applied in online teaching as well.)

Activating long-term memory storage through the spatial domain, where the methodology lives, is "forever learning." Research shows that spatial memory is always there and inexhaustible and is propelled by novelty, discovery, challenge, and the use of metaphors to make learned material personal and reusable. This has been the bedrock of the Design-Based Learning, Backwards Thinking™ method since I began formalizing it in 1969.

> I like Design-Based Learning because it's not just like art. It's more like something never seen so you can actually create something in your mind and bring it to life.
>
> **—Anali He, 4th-grade student,**
> **San Gabriel Unified School District**

SHAPING THE METHODOLOGY

The origins of what grew into the Doreen Nelson Method of Design-Based Learning with its 6½ Steps of Backwards Thinking™ was rooted in my conviction that students could learn to express themselves and become decision-makers able to envision the future and advocate for a healthy, equitable society. What I had to figure out first, however, was key: how to teach students to access the higher-level thinking associated with creative and critical thinking so that they would achieve Non-Specific Transfer of Learning, agilely using and reusing concepts and big topics in different settings. (Much later, I faced a bigger hurdle: how to teach what I had discovered to other teachers.)

I researched learning theory for my master's degree in education to see how experts proposed achieving Non-Specific Transfer of Learning. I looked for answers from my hero educators (John Dewey, Benjamin Bloom, and Jerome Bruner), who wrote about teaching for profound learning. Bruner said that creative thinking was central to the growth of *all* thinking. I found an epiphany in his book, *The Process of Education*, written in 1960 after the then–Soviet Union's launching of Sputnik. Bruner described what was needed in the teaching of math and science if the United States were to move ahead of the Soviets.

He claimed that to do this, educators needed a structure for teaching higher-level, creative thinking. What he said next jumped out at me. "The heart of the creative process," he wrote, was to have "courage of taste," and that educators would have greater knowledge of the entire learning process if it were possible to discover what transpired during what he called "leaps of insight." But, he also wrote that evaluating that would be too hard. Here was my hero telling me that something so important was impossible.

Addressing Bruner's skepticism would become my mission. I would teach creative thinking as a systematic process to activate the higher-level thinking skills that lead to Non-Specific Transfer of Learning. I would teach students how to reason, rather than having them spend most of their instructional time being told what others have reasoned. To capture students' imaginations, I would envision a comprehensive sequence of curriculum-based experiences from simple to complex, set in a "story" sequence that would ask students to imagine, build, and revise original artifacts to display their thinking about serious subject matter. This process, I believed, would make Non-Specific Transfer of Learning easily teachable, would lead to notably improved test scores, meet all of the requirements for college admission, and at the same time promote individuality and self-confidence.

(In December, 2015, I visited Jerome Bruner at his home in New York. Then a remarkable 100-year-old, Jerry said that *The Process of Education* was his most important book, and that "teaching creative thinking is more urgent than ever.")

Bloom's *Taxonomy* describes the teaching of creative thinking and the creation of original things as the culminating goal in educating students. I had been trained to apply the *Taxonomy*, a common resource in teacher training and staff development, by starting with teaching what was needed to meet the strict requirements imposed by fact-based testing. In my early years as a teacher, before I visualized my reverse

"Learning Ladder" in the development of my Backwards Thinking™ method of Design-Based Learning (see Chapter 4), I had followed the prescribed order of the *Taxonomy*, teaching my students to summarize information, to organize what they learned, and to compare and contrast different examples of information that they acquired. Teaching students to become original thinkers with the ability to envision the future was relegated to the end of the learning process, and like most teachers, I had such a full plate that the ultimate goal of eliciting creative thinking became out of necessity, an afterthought.

I began thinking about how I might teach differently to cultivate students' ability to understand, retain, and reuse universal concepts and principles based on Essential Questions in different settings. I wanted learners to think about thinking, to observe their own thought processes, to know what they knew in order to reuse it—to achieve metacognition. I wondered how I could speed up the learning process and get to the end goal of the *Taxonomy* earlier, while systematizing teaching students to become fluid, creative thinkers.

To bring to life the theoretical basis for my master's thesis on Non-Specific Transfer of Learning, I proposed teaching students to make reasoned changes to what already existed so they would gain the ability to transfer learning from one setting to another.

THE CONCEPT OF CHANGE AND NON-SPECIFIC TRANSFER OF LEARNING

In 1968, in my classroom of underserved 5th and 6th graders at Westminster Elementary School in Venice, California, I taught my students that there is a reason that a variety of housing has existed throughout the world by telling them and showing them what tents, teepees, igloos, and skyscrapers have in common. To have my students reach Benjamin Bloom's highest level—imagination and originality—I asked them to consider the environment, the geography, the resources, the attitudes, and technology that make housing what it is now, what it had been since the beginning of time, and what it might be in the future. I wanted them to know that housing is simply a container for human activity and since they were humans, they had the right to think about what that container might be like. I also wanted them to know that every container is human-made or made in nature for a purpose: a house to shelter and protect, a bottle to hold water, a clock to hold time, a pencil to hold lead, an egg to hold life.

This was still a frontward path, but I kept going on it. I obtained donated cameras to have my students photograph their homes. I thought that by looking at and being asked to imagine how to reconfigure where they live, the students would invent their dream houses. Instead, they came back with all kinds of excuses for not doing the assignment. I realized that their homes were not pretty to them and they felt powerless to change their environments.

I showed them how one thing can become another in a dramatic way. I told them how Pop artist Claes Oldenburg had once given an everyday ice bag new meaning in his installation at the American Pavilion at the World's Fair in Osaka, Japan. His enlarged and rotating ice bag was not representative of a giant headache, Oldenburg had explained, but was a symbol of change and dignity as the cap of the bag caught the sun and the bag bowed to the audience as it turned, representing the healing that had taken place between the United States and Japan since World War II.

Close to Halloween, and inspired by Oldenburg, I asked the students to change themselves into an object of their choice by making a "New Skin" costume to create a Never-Before-Seen them. I had them select a small physical object, describe how it symbolized them, and turn it into a body cover. My students chose to be musical instruments, cans of food, bacon and eggs, cameras, wallets, mops, brooms, razor blades, and even a tube of toothpaste. Unexpectedly, I was teaching them to think metaphorically. I had them pretend that they were the objects and use their imaginations to make up stories about what the object did and how it represented who they were.

Non-Specific Transfer of Learning was automatic, and what had started out as an art project had become a backwards path to teaching subject matter. I observed the students' involvement with subject matter lessons and saw that they didn't mind if my list of criteria for their costumes expanded whenever I thought of adding to it. As they built their New Skins, they willingly measured their small, real objects to figure out how many times bigger the objects would need to be to fit as costumes, and what kind of details would make their costumes recognizable. To decide what to use to make their body covers, they debated the difference between using soft fabrics or large rolls of paper versus hard cardboard boxes, and I had them research the costs for each. More Math, Science, and Language Arts lessons emerged. (One student, who had previously refused to read in class at all, managed to copy all of the detailed writing on his soda can and discuss why certain words were on the can in the first place.)

Even those students who had difficulty crafting their New Skins learned to justify their creations. Some students made New Skin body covers that looked better than others, but that wasn't the point. I was teaching them to feel comfortable expressing themselves and leading them to reuse the symbolism and metaphoric thinking inherent in this experience.

It is hard to forget the boy who chose to be a soup can to show that he loved to eat. Or the student who was a razor blade to show his desire to cut things into pieces. Or the girl who was a telephone to represent her fear of having no one to call when she needed a friend.

Dressing up as an object of their choice gave my students the feeling that they had redesigned Halloween. They begged to wear their funny and original New Skin costumes during the school's Halloween parade. They took great pleasure in knowing that everyone else would be the same old skeleton or fairy princess. (Of course, when they did their research about the origins of Halloween, they discovered why certain costumes dominated the holiday.)

Above all, my students were no longer inhibited in imagining themselves as designers. By changing the size and function of an object with intention, and embracing their New Skin selves, they had learned that they had the power to transform one thing into something else. This resulted in a high rate of student success. I had been concerned about justifying having students spend a few hours a day over a three-week period building, wearing, and storing their New Skin body covers, but it proved to be an invaluable use of classroom time, filling a solid month of academic study.

Based on this New Skin activity—the precursor to what would become my methodology's sequential, curriculum-based Design Challenges—my daily Guided Lessons in Math, Science, History, and Language Arts were more comprehensive than any I had been able to teach over my then-10-year career in the classroom.

Seeing how diligently they adhered to the required criteria, I graded them for meeting (or not meeting) what they themselves agreed they needed to achieve. If I had assigned grades for the "best" New Skin, I would have been recognizing them for their motor skills, not for their ability to produce and justify a creative object.

To my surprise, in the longitudinal study I did 10 years after my first New Skin activity in Venice, many of those from that class of students with mixed abilities were in college and still remembered the New Skin objects they had been. Keeping the actual costumes, or photographs of their New Skins was common. I visited two of my former students, siblings, who had moved to Missoula, Montana. In their small house, over the fireplace, hung their 10-year-old New Skin costumes (one was a can of soup).

For some time, I thought that the New Skin activity was the only way to drive home the point that large, student-built artifacts in the classroom made a difference in higher-level learning. I did this activity with students with severe learning disabilities, English Language learners, teachers, lawyers, architects, and computer scientists. After the initial shock of being asked to be silly, none had difficulty in introducing themselves to others as their New Skin selves.

I developed an Object Interview with actors from the Mark Taper Forum, funded by a grant from the National Endowment for the Arts, to apply my methodology to teaching theater to young children. The Object Interview, modeled after what actors do when they take on a role, involves asking a series of questions that interviewers might ask the New Skin Object if they met it on the street. The questions start with the Object's name, where it lives, where it was born, and who its immediate family and distant relatives are. They then move on to the Object's function, what it is good at, scared of, what it dreams about, its social class and economic status—and even what rules and laws govern its existence.

In one 3rd-grade class, eight-year-old Doug Bernstein was a yellow M&M candy, which he remembers to this day. During his Object Interview, he described how happy he was when he was born at the factory and how he had come from a long line of sweets that had made people happy since the beginning of time. Doug said that his relatives ranged from fruit to sugar and that while he loved his M&M family, his favorite thing was to have his owner reach into the bag and choose him. When asked when the M&M would die, Doug put his hands on his head and said, "Oh my god, I was *born* to die." He later wrote a skit about the life cycle of an M&M. (Today, Doug is associate medical director for the Emergency Department at Bon Secours Memorial Regional Medical Center in Richmond, Virginia.)

Although I stopped using the New Skin activity as the gateway to my methodology, many Design-Based Learning teachers I've trained still keep at it. Some body covers are made instantly; others are detailed and precise. Some teachers have students arrange themselves into families of New Skin Objects to make a Venn diagram of similarities and differences. Some teachers create holiday plays, others have students decide which Objects would be the best leaders, based on their Objects' imagined character traits.

In a class I taught at Cal Poly, Pomona, one teacher chose to be a rubber condom. "I'm not a giant prick," he told the class. "I think of myself as a protector, caring for the world." In a Liberal Studies class taught by a History professor I coached, one student presented herself as a chamois cloth. Her husband had chosen that object for her. She said that she was disappointed that he hadn't chosen something more feminine, until he had explained that he thought she was like a chamois cloth because she could be very firm under certain circumstances and soft in others. An engineering major, taking a course in design, made it clear that he felt the New Skin activity was pointless. The day the students were to bring their New Skin selves to class, he was late. He had made himself into a slice of bread covered with peanut butter and jelly, and hadn't been able to get through his front door. He hadn't calculated the dimensions and was forced to dismantle and re-engineer his New Skin in order to bring it to class.

Dan Wishard, an architect in Southern California, was a New Skin student in a 6th-grade class taught by Ruth Hiebert, whom I had trained in my methodology at the Smithsonian Institution in 1972. Dan wrote recently to tell me that he has fond memories of being a

Dan Wishard in his New Skin hammer as a 6th grader in Saugus, California.

hammer one year and a tape dispenser the next: "What an awesome time. I'll never forget it as long as I live," he wrote. "I have told countless people about it and they are always amazed that something like that existed. Looking back, I am, too. What a great experience for all those involved."

The New Skin exercise became personal for me when my step-grandson Jared's other grandmother died and I took him out while his parents made funeral arrangements. We went to see a movie selected by this seven-year-old boy who had a learning disorder and was usually very jumpy, but as we watched the movie, he sat rigid and still. I felt how affected he was by his grandmother's death.

We left the movie and wandered aimlessly through a shopping mall. Tired of it all, I thought of the time Jared had dressed up for Halloween as an Object—a truck costume made by his dad—and I became the educator. I asked Jared, "What if I suddenly turned into my wristwatch?" That hooked him. From then on, I was a wristwatch as he gleefully answered my probing questions about my friends, relatives, my ancestry, enemies, and dreams.

In the Brookstone store, Jared shouted, "Look, there are your relatives!" as he dragged me to see wristwatches, wall clocks, and anything else that ticked or kept time. He explained how each object was like me, but not quite the same. Each store in the mall became a treasure hunt to find a relative, and the relatives got more complex. If they were even made out of the same material as my wristwatch, Jared called them "almost relatives."

I was doing a verbal version of the New Skin activity. I am always struck by the strong attachment that students have to the physical objects that they build in the classroom, but I was surprised by how long Jared wanted to sustain this verbal game. Just before leaving him that night, he said, "So, if you're a wristwatch, when you die, we can just get a new battery and you'll be okay."

His parents said that for the first time in days, Jared went to bed alone that night and slept straight through until morning. Now in his twenties, he still remembers everything about that day.

THE GENESIS OF THE STUDENT-BUILT CITY

I was convinced that teaching students to become creative thinkers had to be integral to all required subjects. I was looking for a way that my method of Design-Based Learning would enable all students— not just those designated as gifted or artistic—to practice creative thinking. If students were asked to design or invent their own solutions to topics and concepts underlying subject matter, *before formally learning that information*, self-expression would bloom and they would become adept in transferring what they learned from one setting to another. They would learn that information was theirs to use and reuse. My research and experience with the New Skin activity had underscored the power of the spatial domain for Non-Specific Transfer of Learning. Now I needed to find a practical way to realize what I had always imagined as the perfect context for learning: a student-built, student-run City of the Future in the classroom, prominent and versatile enough to accommodate the teaching of any subject.

This was on my mind in April 1969, during a trip to Bourton-on-the-Water, an old-world English village tucked away in the Cotswolds, where I walked through a replica of the village built there in 1937 to a one-ninth scale. All of the elements of a real place could be seen at a glance in a tactile example of the power of miniaturization and contextualization. I wondered if my students could build a small City representing their own community, not as it was, but as it might be. The rough artifacts students would make for their City of the Future would not be an end-all. They would be a way for students to think of themselves as inventors, sparking their interest in related subject matter, and motivating them to learn to reason their way to an understanding of how and why a solution to a question or need came about.

I pioneered this process with my "New Skin" students who continued on with me in the 1969–1970 school year. My Westminster Elementary School principal, Sylvia Coop, gave me the green light to teach the yearlong course of study that I was devising for my master's degree using a city as context to promote Non-Specific Transfer of Learning. I team-taught with 3rd- and 4th-grade teacher Ruth Glatt, an artist, sounding board, partner, and friend, who engaged with me and my combined 5th- and 6th-grade class throughout the process. In essence, the existing wall between our classrooms periodically disappeared as collaboration occurred, and over the school year, with contributions from Ruth and her students, my students designed, built, revised, and ran a roughly to-scale City of the Future that represented their Venice, California, community of Oakwood.

To prepare my students to build what they imagined Oakwood would look like 100 years in the future, I first had them locate their homes and local landmarks on a map. We took a field trip to walk around their community with the map so that they would learn what maps were for and how to notice and read details. Back in the classroom, I projected an enlarged map of Oakwood onto a 5- × 7-foot piece of butcher paper and had students trace it.

Because the map was so large, they became actively interested, wanting to know more about how to read a map, why things were where they were, what a legend was, and how maps were made. This led to in-depth Geography lessons that included looking at USGS maps to identify topography and land formations elsewhere. They noticed that their Venice community on the map was flat because it was near the beach. As they looked at different types of maps, they learned that human beings make maps to represent places not easily viewable at a glance. They wrote stories about their existing community. I had them make up word problems related to time and distances between locations. I was able to teach Math, English, Geography, and Science to every type of learner in the class.

I moved the desks to surround a 5 × 7-foot piece of Styrofoam on the floor, topped with our wall map of the Oakwood community, and had the students determine the boundaries for their City of the Future. They outlined Oakwood's main arteries and landmarks on the Styrofoam to make clear that some of what already existed would probably remain in the future for their reinvented community. I put them into Council District groups to simulate a government and had each District make a plan for how to divide the map up so that each student had his or her own piece of "real estate." I taught them how to give oral presentations to justify and advocate for their plans and how to use descriptive language in writing about them. In a City meeting, the whole class voted for the best plan. I cut the Styrofoam into pieces to match the students' agreed-upon plan. Over the next few weeks, as I coupled having students experience democratic decision-making with creative thinking, their inventiveness began to flourish and my Backwards Thinking™ process took form.

After selecting individual land parcels and taking them back to their desks, the student designers had to follow the requirements on my Criteria List. The "Don't Wants" and "Needs" on the Criteria List proved invaluable as a guide, telling students the population of futuristic Oakwood and itemizing the basic needs for any City to be considered a City: shelters, places to exchange goods and services, ways to move around, medical and government services, etc. (This list of needs comes from *The Image of the City* [1960], a seminal work by urban planner, author, and MIT professor Kevin Lynch.)

With the Criteria List as their reference, and my emphasis that their designs not copy what already existed, my students built three-dimensional, very rough models of futuristic houses, power plants, community centers, recreation sites, commercial complexes, and underground and overground ways to move about on their City land parcels. How the finished products looked *didn't matter*. This was to be a Starter City made of recycled materials that students brought to class, to be revised as they studied and applied related subject matter. Ruth Glatt provided tools and techniques that my students used to craft and revise what they envisioned. (It was because of Ruth's ideas that I learned to open up to creative possibilities in my own teaching.)

The Starter City of the Future posed dilemmas that were deliberate in order for students to learn from their mistakes and understand the reasons they would be asked to make revisions. I wanted them to learn to seek and solve problems and persevere by becoming accustomed to constructing original, three-dimensional artifacts that represented their thinking and revising their designs as they collected new information. I wanted them to stop using already existing paradigms. I was determined to have students' original thinking become second nature and visible to them so that they would know what they knew—again, metacognition—and could reuse what they knew.

After my students built what they felt would be needed in their Starter City on their individual land parcels, I had them put the parcels back together on the floor like a giant jigsaw puzzle to teach them how parts make up a whole. This took practice because they had to look at the wall map and rotate the image in their minds to know where to place their land parcels on the physical three-dimensional land site. We had daily races to see who could get his or her piece where it belonged the fastest. I devised all kinds of activities to ensure that everyone knew where their piece of property and everyone else's belonged.

(Looking at a shape in a specific position on a two-dimensional surface and recognizing it in a rotated position is a skill that IQ tests measure, and sure enough, even though IQs were thought to be immutable at the time, this group of underserved students made significant increases. Some went from 90 to 115 on the Individual Stanford-Binet IQ Test.)

When the Styrofoam land parcels were put together, the new dilemma I had planned appeared: the pieces fit, but because the students had been thinking only of what they wanted to build on their own land parcels, there were obvious problems with their designs. They were surprised when they identified how one road ran into the front door of a neighboring property. A freeway abutted a nursery school. There were too many parks and amusement areas and no facilities for the elderly. Some land parcels were dominated by shopping centers with no street access. Overall, there were too few places for living and learning. I guided them to solve this dilemma by having them, over time, do research, revise their designs, and learn to use a government structure to present and justify their solutions.

As my master's degree study of Non-Specific Transfer of Learning took hold, I began to think of ways for students to apply what they learned from building and running their City of the Future to a variety of topics. To connect to the required curriculum, I taught my students to name the problems they identified in their Starter City and associate them with larger topics.

My students gobbled it up. Even my difficult students and slowest learners came to life, creating solutions to the dilemmas they identified that propelled a sequential "story" set within the students' roughly built City in our classroom, based on what they imagined their Venice community would look like in the future.

Connecting the dots between "backwards thinking" and metacognition, instead of starting with the state-mandated K–12 curriculum requirements and textbooks, I developed a sequence of topics and themes around social, political, economic, and environmental issues and constructed a comprehensive course of study encompassing all subjects. For every topic or theme, I had my students build rough artifacts to express their thinking, enabling me to effortlessly engage them in learning what I was required to teach them. The "story" grew each month as I had students imagine and solve different curriculum-related dilemmas in their City of the Future. Built of found materials and governed by students, the City was a visible, daily reminder of their learning. Throughout the school year of building and role-playing, the City became an evolving container for displaying reusable learning across the curriculum.

The artifacts students built for their City became a springboard for lessons in Math, Science, and Language Arts. Without being conscious that they were being taught, my students excelled in presenting their ideas with conviction as they debated with their peers over which design was best for refining their Starter City of the Future and why. What I had hoped came true: my students stopped asking, "Am I doing it right?" and instead learned to assess the plans they made and carried out.

To have my students begin refining their Starter City, I had them study the topic of Shelter. They compared what they had built to types of housing all over the world, learned to describe their buildings in terms of geometric shapes and to calculate size and volume, and revised their designs according to their research. My next topic was Movement. The students compared their designs for moving around their evolving City of the Future and beyond its borders to what they learned about how people throughout history have moved themselves and their necessities. For the topic of Economics and Trade, they redesigned and rebuilt places to buy and sell goods and exchange services. To study Power Sources, my students designed power-saving utilities. To study Health, they built medical services for the citizens of their City, and to learn more about Government Process, they built places to house government services. They built places to store resources, industrial areas, religious facilities, and even places for burials.

When I gave them Pollution as the topic, the students designed ways to get rid of it and did research projects on different forms of pollution (air, land, water, noise, and visual blight). When they wanted a mountain in their City, I had them justify where the soil would come from in their flat community and do science experiments to learn about soil displacement. When they wanted to "demolish" places in present-day Oakwood, I insisted that they figure out where the debris would go. Pretending that a flashlight was the sun shining on their buildings, they learned about the Earth's rotation. When the topic was Efficiency, I taught them about division of labor.

PARALLEL WORLDS

My students spent approximately one month per topic, learning basic subject matter as they went. Regardless of the topic, I made Government and Civics intrinsic to how I taught my students to make connections between their model of a City of the Future and the classroom. To teach about governance and civic responsibility, I had turned the City and the classroom into five corresponding Council Districts and had the students in each District elect representatives. I then rearranged the classroom furniture, grouping tables together to represent each District in the revised City. My students role-played leadership positions in their Council Districts to learn about vested interests. They studied the organization of their community, of Los Angeles, and of the nation. They read the Bill of Rights and parts of the Constitution and wrote about the rights they wanted for their City and their classroom. They began learning the meaning of consequences and to know that laws are enacted for a reason, not simply that laws *are* enacted.

Having my students build and govern their City turned out to be indispensable for my research about Non-Specific Transfer of Learning.

During the months-long process of revising their Starter City of the Future through experiences in critical and creative thinking, students role-played landowners, designers, government officials, and citizens—roles that corresponded to the governance of the classroom.

The students wrote detailed job descriptions and learned to debate such issues as how high the buildings should be in their City of the Future, how the desks should be organized in the classroom, and who got to decide and why. Ultimately, they voted unanimously to have their City remain in the center of the classroom with their desks around it so that they could easily compare their designs to facts they learned about each topic.

My yearlong curriculum became progressively more complex as I presented the sequenced, month-long activities that I would soon call Design Challenges. Based on what I came to call **BIG TOPICS,** these Design Challenges led to my teaching required subjects as Guided Lessons (**small topics**). Having students read, compute, and collect information about what others had done to solve a problem, taught them to make comparisons to their own solutions as they revised their initial designs. My research about the application of Non-Specific Transfer of Learning within the context of a city had come alive.

Experiencing higher-level Non-Specific Transfer of Learning, my students easily absorbed information and applied it to new situations. They were exactly where I wanted them to be. They became detectives, uncovering ways that changes in housing occur because of natural conditions—earthquakes, weather changes—or because of poverty, human interventions, and inventions. They freely projected themselves into the future, imagining change from their own perspectives. It was obvious that my students had gained a sense of power over their learning. They loved that there were so many ways to be "right" and I did, too. As their City of the Future came to life, we all became a family of learners.

Over the months, my students made significant gains in their academic skills. This propelled me to go on to explore ways to deepen the understanding and practice of Non-Specific Transfer of Learning through my gradually evolving 6½ Steps of Backwards Thinking™, the heart of my Design-Based Learning methodology.

I discovered that what I called things mattered. To avoid starting at the lowest level on *Bloom's Taxonomy* with what is known, I asked for Never-Before-Seen everything. They built Never-Before-Seen Creatures to learn about the characteristics of animals, Never-Before-Seen Shelters to learn about protection, Never-Before-Seen Ways to Move People and Goods around the City—and later, a Never-Before-Seen Way to Transmit Disease to study a viral vector.

For each experience, I gave the students a checklist of specific criteria that I derived from subject requirements. These defined the conditions they needed to meet to achieve their designs. Real designers always have constraints—from the client, from government regulations, or from the description of the design problem itself. Artists and scientists work within a set of constraints, too. When I gave my students my Criteria List, I was the client.

I taught them to describe their design solutions orally in different settings (one-on-one, in small groups, and to the entire class), to learn to own what they had made. My students grew so attached to their creations that they wanted to read, research, and write about how what they made compared to real-life solutions—and they frequently said that their solutions were better!

None of these student-made designs required elaborate materials or inordinate classroom time. The initial Never-Before-Seen designs were "instant" physical representations of students' creative thinking, built in only 30 to 45 minutes. The result was as simple as a piece paper turned into a three-dimensional artifact. Having it, being able to describe the thought process that got them there, then refining their initial creations with new vocabulary associated with the design dilemma, led my students to learn required information and remember it.

While my students were applying creative thinking to the design of physical artifacts for their City, Ruth's 3rd and 4th graders expressed their creativity in filmmaking: their documentary-style film, *The History of Oakwood,* about the real Oakwood community, won a prize at a children's film festival.

In my longitudinal study 10 years later, when I made a film (*Classroom City*) surveying students from my 1969–1970 class, a nonreader had become the editor of the student paper at the University of California at Santa Cruz, a once-average student was an attorney, a shy girl (who was removed from her abusive home and placed in foster care while in the class) became a published author and based many of her stories around that time period.

My research from my class in Venice, and my subsequent experience in training K–12 teachers in cross-curricular "City Building" gave me a comprehensive template for teaching the theoretical underpinnings of what would become the Doreen Nelson Method of Design-Based Learning with 6½ Steps of Backwards Thinking™.

I had been searching for a limitless context. The City was it.

LESSONS ALONG THE WAY

Iconic designers Ray and Charles Eames, whose Venice, California, office was across the street from Westminster Elementary School when I was teaching there, discovered my work in 1971. After showing their films and pictures of their furniture to my students, I wrote and asked the Eameses to come to see the "City of the Future" that my students had built, based on the Oakwood area of Venice that included their office. The busy designers politely declined. Undaunted, my students, whom I had taught to advocate for themselves, wrote a giant, knock-out of a letter, complete with drawings of their City, and delivered it in person to the Eames Office. Ray and Charles showed up the next day and, after witnessing my methodology in action, saw to it that I received National Endowment for the Arts funding (Charles was on the board of the NEA). They took 6,000 slides of classrooms for a visual presentation and a film about my methodology as I trained other teachers in diverse neighborhoods, and gave me space in the Eames Office for the making of a film about my methodology.

Some years later, I mentioned to Ray Eames with pride how, early in 1971, I had taught my 4th and 5th graders in Venice about the art of American painter, sculptor, and printmaker Frank Stella and taken them to an exhibit of his work at the Pasadena Art Museum (now the Norton Simon Museum).

I was married to an art dealer then and we lived upstairs from his cutting-edge Los Angeles art gallery, so I was surrounded by such artists as Stella, Claes Oldenburg, Robert Indiana, Ed Ruscha, John Chamberlain, John Altoon, Edward Keinholz, H. C. "Cliff" Westermann, and Louise Nevelson. Taking my students to see art exhibitions had become part of my regular teaching practice. I hoped to inspire them to think creatively and to be creative, so for each new exhibit, I wracked my brain trying to figure out how to prepare them for what they would see.

(After one such excursion to the Pasadena Art Museum to see a show about the Bauhaus School, as the bus drove home to Venice through downtown Los Angeles, one of my students pointed to the skyscrapers and yelled, "Look! Bauhaus is everywhere!")

By the time the Frank Stella exhibit came to Pasadena, I had conceived my Design-Based Learning methodology. Wanting to teach my students that artists were not a rarified group, I decided not to first show them Stella's work, but to have them "invent" what it was like being him.

I moved all of the desks in the classroom to the side and brought in large rolls of white butcher paper, bottles of brightly colored tempera paint, and scale-enlarged compasses and protractors. I told my students that they could do anything they wanted to do, but they had to use the tools that I had provided. My hope was that they would make giant and bold geometrical paintings that resembled Frank Stella's work. That's exactly what happened. They even trimmed the butcher paper where paint had been applied sloppily, with results similar to Stella's shaped canvases. (One student, instead of making art, went to the library—with my permission—and ended up writing a lengthy report on the history and function of the compass and protractor.)

After my students completed their projects, I brought them to the Stella Exhibit at the Museum, where the Grinstein Family, cofounders of the renowned Gemini G.E.L. artists' workshop, arranged to have my students meet Frank Stella and show him their work.

Stella greeted my students, who eagerly unrolled their large paintings for his perusal and happily accepted his compliments. When they saw Stella's own work, they could not contain themselves. "He stole our ideas!" they exclaimed. All of the adults in attendance were enchanted by this reaction and by what the students had painted.

In relating all of this to Ray Eames (who was herself a painter), I was sort of patting myself on the back, telling her how I had empowered my students to think like artists. When I finished the story, Ray smiled and said gently, "Yes, but they didn't learn how Frank Stella *knew* to use those instruments, those geometric shapes, bright colors, and to shape his large canvases. That," she said, "is the real struggle: to find one's own voice."

I realized then that I had unintentionally tricked my students into replicating Stella's artwork, contradicting my intended goal: to enable students to achieve higher-level learning through original, creative thinking.

THE SMITHSONIAN

A significant "aha" moment for me occurred in 1971 at the Smithsonian, where I began to dig deeper into how to teach my methodology to others. In the spring of that year my brother, Frank Gehry, was asked by the director of the Smithsonian Institution Associates to teach a class for middle school students with a woman whose classroom in Venice, California, had been featured as part of a recent ABC Network Christmas Eve special about envisioning the future in America.

Frank had no idea that I was the woman the director was talking about . . . and I had no idea that while I was having my students build a City in my classroom in Venice, Frank had been teaching kids about cities in an after-school class called "Fantastic Cities" at Barnsdall Park in Los Angeles.

When we teamed up, Frank and I decided that since we had both built cities with kids, we would do that at the Smithsonian, although our motivations differed. Frank thought of the city as a palette for creative thinking about the built environment; I was fixated on the City as a tool for the transference of learning.

We wanted to have fun together, so on the plane to Washington, we made up a story about a miracle element that would save the world from pollution. We called this element "Purium," and in a dark basement room of the Castle Building at the Smithsonian, we told the middle school students there that they were agents of the government assigned to build and govern a City of the Future for a population that would mine, process, and ship the "Purium."

The director of the Smithsonian provided an array of arts and crafts materials. The teacher in me insisted that the kids refer to a Criteria List of "Don't Wants" and "Needs" so that they would have a tool to evaluate their creations. (The Criteria List is like having another teacher in the classroom. I tell teachers that when their students want to know if what they are doing is "right," just point to the list and ask them to read it themselves to see if they have met the criteria. This ensures that students learn the vocabulary that their teacher wants them to learn.)

At the Smithsonian, four hours later, Frank asked the students what they wanted to do with the "instant City" they had built.

"Tear it down!" was the response.

I was horrified. Trash their City? That went against everything that I had been taught about having students value their work. I worried, too, about how the students might reuse this experience in the future. But the kids tore into what they had built, screaming with high-pitched glee, and when Frank asked if they wanted to build another one, the answer was a loudly enthusiastic, "YES!"

"Do you think it will be better?" he asked. Another resounding, "YES!"

It struck me then that the destructive forces in nature are germinal to creation, and that if I were truly serious about teaching kids to think creatively, allowing them to "destroy" and then revise their original products—after an evaluation—could be central to their refinement of their own creative works.

I've never forgotten those gleeful shouts that day at the Smithsonian. When the same vocal enthusiasm occurs in Design-Based Learning classrooms, as students build, and then revise and refine their solutions to Design Challenges, it is invariably the harbinger of deliberate creative action.

Psychologist Abraham Maslow, creator of Maslow's Hierarchy of Needs, said, "If you only have a hammer, you tend to see every problem as a nail." The flip side is that if you're taught to think creatively, you invent another tool to solve the problem. This tenet is fundamental to my method of Design-Based Learning.

THE CITY

A Limitless Context for Teaching and Learning

A desirable, sustainable world for ourselves and our children in 2046 cannot be predicted, and certainly will not be achieved by default. It can be achieved by design, as designers of the future apply their talent and enthusiasm to the task.

—Inventor and aeronautical engineer Paul B. McCready, "Design in 2046," *Design News Magazine,* **November 4, 1996**

"Do we actually have to build a City of the Future in the classroom?" This is a question I have fielded over decades of training teachers in the methodology.

The answer is yes. Or, if not a City of the Future, any other contextual, three-dimensional, tabletop model of an imagined, built environment. This is the gestalt: the whole City is greater than its individual parts. The City functions as a metaphor for the interconnectedness of all subject matter.

My research, across the years and across grade levels, is definitive. A tabletop, Never-Before-Seen Starter City of the Future (or Community, Settlement/Colony, Ancient Civilization, Biome, Biosphere, Business, or any other curriculum-based, contextual environment representing a real place or system) is a time-limited plunge into the totality of The Doreen Nelson Method of Design-Based Learning.

Building and running a Never-Before-Seen, three-dimensional world is purposeful play as students role-play as planners, land developers, designers, and government representatives. As builders, government officials, and citizens of the City, they are encouraged to invent and bring to life whatever their minds can envision. The whirlwind activity of building a Starter City of the Future is noisy, messy, and engaging and gives learners an experience of creation they'll never forget. Completed under time pressure, it provides a setting for students to analyze their omissions and mistakes. They learn to problem seek and problem solve as the teacher prepares them to slow down, develop, and run the City, refining it over a semester or school year by responding to a sequence of **BIG TOPIC** Design Challenges that lead to **small topic** Guided Lessons. (A teacher might say, "You're going to be building and running a Starter City and it will change as you learn more.")

RUNNING AND REFINING A NEVER-BEFORE-SEEN (NBS) STARTER CITY OF THE FUTURE: AN EXAMPLE OF 10 DESIGN CHALLENGES HIGHLIGHTING CIVICS AND GOVERNANCE

ESSENTIAL QUESTION	How do humans organize living together?	How do humans represent themselves and communicate their values to others?
BIG TOPIC	CONTEXT	IDENTITY
DESIGN CHALLENGE	#1 NBS Starter City (or any other contextual environment)	#2 NBS Avatar/Creature
3-D	• Build a NBS Starter City with an odd number of Council Districts (to break voting ties)	• Build an Instant NBS Avatar/Creature
TEACHER'S CRITERIA LIST	• A Criteria List with requirements	• A Criteria List with requirements

COUNCIL DISTRICT MEETINGS	• Role-play Council District Leaders and Commissioners • Identify the most urgent City problem • Make rules for how to solve the problem • Prepare to present the most urgent problem and rules for a solution	• Introduce Avatar/Creatures to each other • Explain how assigned roles differ from one another • Practice the roles
CITY MEETINGS FOR MAKING DECISIONS	• Mayor invites each Council District to present and justify its most urgent problem and rules for a solution • Vote on the single most urgent problem for the City as a whole and what rules will be applied to solve the problem (Shelter)	• Each Council District presents its members and their roles

GUIDED LESSONS	• Read about how a real city government and its officials work (Mayor, Council District Leaders, Commissioners, etc.)	• Name existing government documents that establish rules and regulations (Bill of Rights, Constitution).
	• Role-play Commissioners of Protection/Equity, Mobility, Trade/Commerce, Culture/Education, Power, Sanitation, Social Services, Health/Well-Being	• Identify the vocabulary and protocol for meetings (Roberts Rules of Order)
	• Discuss the function of each role	• Summarize assigned job descriptions in writing
	• Write job descriptions	• Discuss, summarize and agree on how to make decisions as a group
	• Write applications for the preferred job	• Plan length of City Meetings (5 minutes), how to run a meeting, how to take notes, how to listen, how to ask questions, how to record time, and how to vote
		• Make wearable symbols to visually identify assigned roles

	PROTECTION/EQUITY	MOBILITY
ESSENTIAL QUESTION	How do humans humanely shelter and protect themselves and others from natural or human made phenomena to survive and equitably coexist?	How do humans move across terrains in a just and environmentally responsible way?
BIG TOPIC	PROTECTION/EQUITY	MOBILITY
DESIGN CHALLENGE	#3 NBS Shelter to protect from natural or human made phenomena	#4 NBS Carrier and Movement System
3-D	• Build a NBS Shelter	• Build a NBS Carrier and Movement System
TEACHER'S CRITERIA LIST	• A Criteria List with requirements	• A Criteria List with requirements
COUNCIL DISTRICT MEETINGS	• Continue role-playing jobs • Discuss the meaning of humanizing a shelter, including size, height and function (to protect from natural or human made phenomena) • Identify and prepare to present main requirements for Shelters at the City Meeting	• Present built Carriers and Movement Systems • Decide as a District which Carriers and Movement Systems to present at the City Meeting and justify why • Decide on rules and regulations regarding mobility, accessibility, and equity

CITY MEETINGS FOR MAKING DECISIONS	
• Each Council District presents its solutions for making revisions to humanize their Shelters, including scale, size, height, and function • Vote on requirements for Shelters to be included in the City to humanize and protect citizens.	• Each Council District presents its Carriers and Movement Systems • Vote on which Carriers and Movement Systems to build for the City • Each Council District presents its rules and regulations regarding mobility • Vote on which rules and regulations will govern mobility in the City

GUIDED LESSONS	
• Give examples of what it means to humanize a Shelter, ensure equity, accessibility, and protect citizens from natural and human made phenomena • Identify main elements and functions of a Shelter: the amount of space needed for each • Distinguish between different kinds of historic and contemporary Shelters (cave, wagon, dugout, tent, mobile dwelling. house, apartment building, prison etc.) • Define similarities, differences, adaptations among Shelters throughout history and in various geographic locations	• Read about Carriers and Movement Systems throughout history and how they have impacted different populations and the environment • Identify problems limiting Movement in cities—locally, statewide, nationally, and internationally • Make decisions to equitably apply rules and regulations about mobility • Research the costs of building and maintaining infrastructure • Research how infrastructure is funded among city, state, and federal governments

	• Compare and contrast differences among NBS Shelters to determine if they are humane • Justify the size of spaces within each Shelter • Judge the environmental impact of single Shelters verses multi- Shelters, and small verses tall Shelters	• Read about how geographical location affects governmental decisions about infrastructure • Research Movement Systems in students' own community (cost and frequency of public transport)
ESSENTIAL QUESTION	How do humans exchange goods and services needed for survival while supporting equitable access and division of labor?	How do humans get and distribute energy in an equitable and socially responsible way?
BIG TOPIC	TRADE/COMMERCE	ENERGY/POWER
DESIGN CHALLENGE	#5 NBS Places to Exchange Goods and Services	#6 NBS Places and Ways to Equitably Get and Distribute Energy
3-D	• Build a NBS Place to Exchange Goods and Services	• Build NBS Places and Ways to Equitably Get and Distribute Energy
TEACHER'S CRITERIA LIST	• A Criteria List with requirements	• A Criteria List with requirements

COUNCIL DISTRICT MEETINGS	• Present built Places to Exchange Goods and Services • Decide as a District which Places to present at the City Meeting and why • Develop an equitable division of labor plan for exchanging goods and services • Prepare to present the plan at the City Meeting • Make rules and regulations regarding trade and commerce • Prepare to present the rules and regulations at the City Meeting	• Present built Places and Ways to Equitably Get and Distribute Energy • Decide as a District which Places and Ways to present at the City Meeting to be included in the City and why • Prepare to present at the City Meeting the selected Places and Ways to get and distribute services throughout the City
CITY MEETINGS FOR MAKING DECISIONS	• Each Council District presents its Places to Exchange Goods and Services. • Vote on which Places to include in the City • Each Council District presents its rules and regulations regarding trade and commerce • Vote on rules and regulations to govern trade and commerce in the City • Each Council District presents its plan for equitable division of labor • Vote on which plan for an equitable division of labor will be used to govern trade and commerce in the City	• Each Council District presents its Places and Ways to Equitably get and Distribute Energy • Vote on the number of Places and Ways to be included in the City • Vote on and select which Places and Ways will be included in the City

GUIDED LESSONS	• Read about systems of trade and commerce around the world • Research how rules and regulations regarding trade and commerce have changed throughout history • Discuss how rules and regulations regarding trade and commerce affect division of labor and worker rights and safety. • Research underserved communities	• Read about various Places and Ways that Energy is produced and distributed to citizens • Discuss the pros and cons of various forms of Energy • Research factors that limit accessibility to Energy • Read about how various forms of Energy have affected the health of citizens
ESSENTIAL QUESTION	How do the arts, humanities, and sciences promote a civilized society?	How do humans responsibly and justly maintain cleanliness while protecting the global environment?
BIG TOPIC	**CULTURE/ EDUCATION**	**SANITATION**
DESIGN CHALLENGE	#7 NBS Places for Learning and Cultural Exchange	#8 NBS Environmentally Responsible Sanitation System and Places for Waste Collection and Disposal

3-D	• Build NBS Places for Learning and Cultural Exchange	• Build a NBS Environmentally Responsible Sanitation System and Places for Waste Collection and Disposal
TEACHER'S CRITERIA LIST	• A Criteria List with requirements	• A Criteria List with requirements
COUNCIL DISTRICT MEETINGS	• Present built Places for Learning and Cultural Exchange • Discuss and vote on whether Places for culture and learning should be separate or combined • Vote on Places to present at the City Meeting and justify why • Prepare to present to the City Meeting	• Each Council District presents its Environmentally Responsible Sanitation System and Places for Waste Collection and Disposal • Discuss and vote on whether those Systems and Places should be separate or combined • Vote which Systems and Places will be included in the City and justify why • Prepare to present to the City Meeting
CITY MEETINGS FOR MAKING DECISIONS	• Each Council District presents its Places for Education and Cultural Exchange • Vote on whether Places for culture and learning should be separate or combined • Vote on which Places will be included in the City	• Each Council District presents its System and Places for Waste Collection and Disposal • Vote on which System and Places to build in the City

GUIDED LESSONS	• Research the origins of formal education • Read about how knowledge is passed on (the written word, visually, storytelling) • Discuss how the arts foster self-expression and lead to new ways of thinking • Research Places where art made and displayed • Research factors that limit accessibility to education and opportunities for cultural growth • Read about how and why some works of literature, visual art, and music have been banned by governments past and present • Research how Places for Learning and Cultural Exchange are funded	• Read about the history of sanitation, from the origins of civilization to space travel • Discuss how new scientific breakthroughs and global warming inform the need for alternative ways and places to dispose of waste • Research factors that limit opportunities for sanitation • Research why some pollutants have been banned by governments past and present. • Read about the costs of creating a clean environment
ESSENTIAL QUESTION	How do humans protect and care for all members of society?	How do humans maintain their physical and mental health?
BIG TOPIC	SOCIAL SERVICES, HEALTH & WELFARE	WELL-BEING
DESIGN CHALLENGE	#9 NBS Places with Services to Protect and Care for Others	#10 NBS Places and Ways to Provide Physical and Emotional Well-Being

3-D	• Build NBS Places with Services to Protect and Care for Others	• Build NBS Places and Ways to Provide Physical and Emotional Well-Being
TEACHER'S CRITERIA LIST	• A Criteria List with requirements	• A Criteria List with requirements
COUNCIL DISTRICT MEETINGS	• Each District presents its built Places with Services to Protect and Care for Others • Decide if Places with Services should be separate or combined. • Decide as a District which Places with Services to present at the City Meeting and why	• Each District presents its built Places and Ways to Provide Physical and Emotional Well-Being Decide if Places and Ways should be separate or combined • Decide as a district which Places and Ways to present to the City meeting and why
CITY MEETINGS FOR MAKING DECISIONS	• Each Council District presents its Places and Services to Protect and Care for Others • Vote on which Places with Service should be included in the City	• Each Council District presents its Places and Ways to Provide Physical and Emotional Well-Being • Vote on whether Places and Ways should be separate or combined and justify why • Vote on which Places and Ways should be included in the City

GUIDED LESSONS	• Read about history and laws related to how governments have cared for citizens in need (hospitals, rehabilitation centers, nursing homes, daycare, eldercare, prisons, etc.) • Discuss how new scientific/medical discoveries affect the cost of health care • Research the need for alternative ways and places to care for or rehabilitate citizens (including those in need inside prisons) • Research factors that limit opportunities for protection and care • Read about the costs of creating Places with Services to care for others • Research why past and present governments became involved in providing care and rehabilitation for citizens • Discuss the importance of caring for others and how various cultures pass these values on from one generation to the next	• Read about how the lack of open space and green space in communities affects the health and well being of citizens • Research health implications of limited access to places of exercise and recreation • Survey local communities to determine the number and availability of parks, other recreational facilities, and green space in general

A sampling of curriculum-based BIG TOPICS related to a city or other contextual environments:

- **COMPLEXITY/DIVERSITY:** A city is a complex and diverse entity.

- **SUSTAINABILITY:** A city provides basic needs—shelter, food, water, transportation—and other vital services.

- **INTERCONNECTEDNESS:** The whole is greater than the sum of its parts.

- **GOVERNANCE:** Building a city requires planning, cooperation, and decision-making.

- **ENTROPY:** The pressure of circumstance produces change, whether planned for or not.

- **ADAPTABILITY:** People invent the city, and they can adapt and transform it.

- **ORGANIZATION:** A charted plan is based on knowing specifically what is not wanted, what is needed, and how to get it.

- **PERSEVERANCE:** Goals can be achieved by following a plan of action.

When students roughly build a tabletop City in the classroom, they begin with individual land parcels that they will develop together into a whole through playing various government roles. The land parcels are pieces of cardboard or foam board approximately 12 by 16 inches. (These land parcels can be larger or smaller depending on grade level. For distance learning, students' land parcels need to be large enough to be visible to all online.)

By role-playing a City government, students learn to collaborate and communicate as they problem-solve how to join their pieces together, either in the classroom or virtually. This gives them significant buy-in to subject matter and civic, social, and emotional

A student in Georgia Singleton's 4th-grade class holding the individual land parcel she built for the tabletop City's Council District B2.

Georgia Singleton's 4th-grade students proudly display their tabletop City after succeeding in joining their individual land parcels together.

learning across the curriculum. I have tried to teach the methodology to teachers without a City. I even applied the methodology to develop a theater program, a marine biology program, and a law-related education program. Some of these efforts seemed to work at first, but fizzled due to a lack of comprehensive context. Nothing has replaced having K–12 students build and run a representation of a City of the Future or other imagined, dynamic environment based on a real location or system, in the classroom or in an online setting.

THE VERSATILITY OF THE CITY

I am convinced that the work of building a sense of social responsibility is one of the biggest priorities of most educational leaders. Design-Based Learning brings the elements of exploration, critical thinking, planning, and building to not just support curriculum and standards, but to instill a sense of cooperation and mutual responsibility, and the ability to identify and develop solutions to problems of learning, life, and community in a way like nothing I have seen.

—**Jeff Seymour, Professor, Cal Poly Pomona; former Superintendent, El Monte City School District, September 2019**

Teachers delivering their curricula through the Design-Based Learning methodology have amplified the 6th-grade study of ancient civilizations by having students build and govern environments fueled by a "story" that they are the first people to experience the dawn of civilization. Fourth- and 5th-grade teachers teaching about American Expansion and the development of settlements have had their students imagine themselves as the first people to travel across unfamiliar, pre-industrial terrain and build and run a settlement. High school students have built imagined biological environments to learn about genetics and evolution, and small islands to learn about the origins of conflict in World History.

Having students roughly build a City of the Future or comparable environment in the physical classroom (or in a hybrid combination of virtual and in-person learning) to trigger their research and textbook study gives them a three-dimensional sketch of their thinking. They hold the key to labeling the parts, are able to explain the purpose of their built creations, and through a government structure learn to make revisions based on factual information and consensus. Learning takes on personal meaning and is stored in students' long-term memories as they become invested in their own constructed artifacts.

During all the years that I've had pre-K through 12th-grade teachers and university faculty (as well as lawyers, designers, marine biologists, and computer scientists) build a City as part of their training in the methodology, whether we meet in person or online, I have never been bored looking at and listening to descriptions of what people of any age build and the problems they identify and want to solve. No one else is ever bored, either. Everyone wants to talk about what they build for their City and comment on and question the designs and proposals of others. A student-built, student-run tabletop City is a container of diverse information, a perfect metaphor for teaching and learning anything. It can represent a specific neighborhood, community, city, business, nation, planet, or biological system. It can amplify any topic, any concept, any principle, and any Essential Question.

Having K–12 students build, run, and refine a City in the classroom or online gives everyone the same reference point. Whether we realize it or not, we are always comparing any unfamiliar city to our own. Looking at a "newly" student-designed City invites the same kind of comparisons. The roughly built City is a mini-world, a laboratory, and a teacher's platform for integrating the curriculum, applying civics education, and having students practice, test, and refine their creative and critical thinking skills.

When I began training other teachers in the methodology, I was not always successful at explaining to them or to school administrators that a City built in a 3rd-grade classroom would serve different purposes than one built by 6th graders or high school students. Because at the time I was calling it an "Instant City," teachers tended to think of it as a discrete, hands-on project to be finished and done with when time was up. I didn't realize that it was my own terminology that was contributing to this lack of understanding.

"You tell us that what a Design Challenge is called matters," a teacher said to me one day. "When we hear 'Instant City,' we think of it as the kind of short-term project we're used to."

She was right. Once I began calling the "Instant City" a "Starter City," teachers immediately understood that the initial construction of a City was simply the first step in a continuing sequence of curriculum-based Design Challenges.

I cannot stress enough that the student-built City is not an arts-and-crafts project to be judged for its aesthetic quality. Nor is it a lesson in architecture or urban planning. A student-built City is a simulated experience that takes place over time as students respond to a series of Design Challenges to build Never-Before-Seen Creatures/ Avatars, Shelters, Ways to Move, Places for Commerce, Medical Services, Government Services, Education, Recreation, and Waste Disposal, Ways to Avoid Pollution, etc. Although the word "avatar" was not in the vocabulary at the time, my students in the 1960s and 1970s behaved then as students do now in any grade level: as if they were playing a serious, ongoing game with their "Avatars" in charge.

It is the process of building, governing, and refining a City, not the end result, that gives students practice with "what if" and "why," inspiring problem-solving, creativity, and higher-level thinking.

Crumpled, twisted, or rolled pieces of paper; folded pieces of cardboard, lumps of clay shaped by students' hands, are filled with meaning, emotions, descriptions, and stories. The concepts that these artifacts represent become embedded in students' brains.

Every day, when the City is prominent in the physical or virtual learning environment, students can't help but think about what they made, what their peers made, and what they will discuss in their Council District and City Meetings. As the teacher deepens their understanding of what they have made by having them study required subject matter topics, they are eager to revisit their choices and revise their creations. The City becomes a daily reminder to students that they are creative thinkers and gives them a compelling reason for learning basic subject skills, including presentation, speaking, listening, and writing. (Describing my work, designer Charles Eames said, "You don't have to bring a symphony orchestra or a dance troupe into the classroom to inspire students to be creative. You just give them a context, a City, for playing out their original ideas.")

To this day, since my early research began, when I see unengaged students, ask them to solve a Design Challenge, and give them a piece of paper to turn into an artifact that shows their thoughts, they come to life. Unlike most artifacts that students make and take home and never use again, what they create for their City, in the classroom or online, grows in complexity and increasingly showcases and reviews their learning.

My Design-Based Learning methodology has the same learning goals and objectives as traditional methodologies, but it starts by focusing on the students' initial knowledge of a topic, not by telling or showing them "this is how it is done in textbooks." Instead, students come up with their own solutions for each problem that they identify in their City and present for a vote in their simulated government, adhering to the vocabulary for what is to be studied. Higher-level learning begins immediately with the building of a creative artifact that is refined through subsequent learned information.

Design-Based Learning K–12 teachers continually prove the effectiveness and flexibility of the methodology in achieving Non-Specific Transfer of Learning in ways I never imagined, in the physical classroom and in the virtual world.

IN THE CLASSROOM

In some years, you will have a different experience with the same music.

—Igor Stravinsky, in the 1982 documentary *Stravinsky: Once at a Border*, directed by Tony Palmer

Creature Land (2nd Grade)

Fontana Unified School District Principal Terry Ceja, who graduated in 1999 from the Design-Based Learning master's degree program at Cal Poly Pomona, taught 2nd grade in an underserved community in the Hacienda-La Puente Unified School District. Terry had her students begin by designing Never-Before-Seen Creatures that would live in a City and need to have shelter, find food, and protect themselves from natural and human-made disasters.

She developed a yearlong study called Creature Land with a series of 10 Design Challenges that she presented to her students to teach them the required curriculum. Terry began with a lesson in symbolism. She had her students make rough paper models of a hand-held object that they felt represented their personality. These small paper models became the students' Creatures/Avatars. To further encourage their personal ownership, Terry even had the students dress up as their Creatures in costumes they made out of butcher paper and painted. (These included "Pencil Girl," "Wristwatch Boy," and "Telephone Man.")

For the next Design Challenge, students created Never-Before-Seen Shelters for their City, Creature Land, to protect their small Creatures from what they decided would be the "scariest" threat, be it water, an earthquake, "mean people," or wild animals.

Enchanted by their creations, Terry's students willingly learned the required subjects. They read about topics related to their creations—animals, protection, transportation, etc.—compared their designs to what they learned, and wrote descriptive stories. They measured their creations and studied maps to find a real place for the tabletop world they were building.

I visited Terry's class with the noted educator and writer Herb Kohl. The students greeted us, asking what object *we* were, because their teacher told them that everyone is like a special object. They went on to describe all of the members of the mini-society they were governing, and although different, all of their Creatures had learned to get along, they said.

Future City (2nd Grade)

Miguel Fernandez was a 2nd-grade teacher in the Pomona Unified School District when he entered the master's program at Cal Poly in 1995 in the second cohort group. Although he never graduated due to a family tragedy, Miguel always had his students build and run a Future City in his classroom until his retirement in 2006. He was naturally theatrical, using his talent to create events that required his students' immediate action in Future City: an earthquake to teach about earthquake preparedness, a person new to the City needing a place to live to teach about immigration and cultural differences.

When his students designed a place to keep wild animals across a river to protect people living in Future City, Miguel told them that a big, mean bird had flown across their river. He asked them, "What do you think might happen?" His students said the mean bird might eat

(Top) A real location is redesigned by 2nd-grade students and called Creature Land. (Bottom) Learning Math through Creature Land.

someone in the City. Miguel asked, "How can you change your design to keep that from happening?" In response, his students invented an enclave that contained the animals and protected the people.

Their interest was high as they studied the natural food chain. Miguel's evolving Future City "story" captured his students' imagination so thoroughly that they excelled at what they needed to learn.

Morality as a Topic (11th-Grade English)

High school English teacher Grace Lim Hays, who graduated from the Design-Based Learning master's degree program at Cal Poly in 2004 and taught the methodology in that program and at ArtCenter College of Design, instructed her 11th graders in the Walnut Valley Unified School District to build a three-dimensional City on a table at the back of the class-room. She referred to it regularly as the context for a series of Design Challenges to develop topics and central themes found in the required texts.

I visited Grace's classroom one day with Betty Ortiz (the wife of Cal Poly's president, J. Michael Ortiz). I had explained that the students were studying Nathaniel Hawthorne's classic, *The Scarlet Letter*, using my methodology and that before having them read the book, with its archaic language that most students would find difficult, Grace had them explore the topic of morality as a theme by building a Never-Before-Seen Place for Promoting Morality in their City.

I told Betty that Grace had given her students a Criteria List with all of the constraints that came directly from the text to prepare them for the vocabulary they would be encountering. That Criteria List asked for reasons that someone would be sent to this Never-Before-Seen Place and required students to explain what happened to people there, how long they stayed, what they did while they were there, what they did when they left, and how the Place and those sent there were seen by others on the "outside." I explained that Grace used the Criteria List to hold students accountable for what they built.

Betty was as surprised as I had been to hear that Grace's students had first designed extremely cruel Places. The class had voted to adopt the plan that gave everyone in the City a brain implant and had them monitored and zapped by a central power if they thought or did anything that was on the students' list of things that were "not nice." Grace told me that once her students began reading *The Scarlet Letter*, they were mesmerized—and that when she had them compare what they had designed as their Places for Promoting Morality to what Hawthorne had written, her students were appalled. She told me they said that what they had built was "even meaner" than what they had read about in the book and that they didn't want a society or a city that operated that way.

The day that Betty and I visited, Grace's students were in groups, discussing ways to revise what they had designed. They then presented their proposals to the whole class. After a vote, the students concluded that they wanted gentle places for promoting morality, places for rehabilitation, and places where citizens aired their individual and group preferences. Every step of the way, as they revised their designs, the students made comparisons between what they had first proposed and their revisions, then wrote about their designs, their opinions, and their comparisons. One student came up to me on his way out the door and said, "I hated reading before this class."

(Grace told me that when her students went on to read *To Kill a Mockingbird*, they didn't have to build anything more in their City because the topic of morality was fresh for them and they easily compared both books. On their formal High School Exit Writing Test, she reported, her students received the highest scores in the school.)

Organic City: "Seeing the Unseen" (12th-Grade Biology)

Richard Rosa, a teacher in the Pasadena Unified School District, graduated from the Design-Based Learning master's degree program in 2014 and earned a doctorate degree in Education Leadership. Rosa, like Grace Lim Hays, taught the methodology at Cal Poly Pomona and at ArtCenter College of Design. He wrote about the experience that one of his high school AP Biology classes had with building and governing a tabletop City.

"I implemented the Design-Based Learning methodology in a curriculum I developed to teach students about the evolution and survival of life on Earth. I called this curriculum Organic City, since all living things are composed of organic materials. I challenged my students to design and build three-dimensional, Never-Before-Seen Creatures/Avatars. These were to represent living things with specific characteristics and traits: the ability to respond and adapt to their environment, take in energy, expel waste, grow and change during varying stages of their life cycles, reproduce, and have multiple structures with varying functions. To ensure that their Creatures could survive, my students had to adhere to this Criteria List.

"I didn't tell them where their Creatures came from. I had my students build a Never-Before-Seen Landsite and Never-Before-Seen Shelters on a table in the back of the classroom as a living environment for their Creatures. In order to understand how genetics determine evolution, my students studied the function of DNA and I asked them to assign a code to their Creatures for a very specific defense mechanism: a particular scent to ward off predators. I brought in a fragrance expert to tell students about how perfumes are made and why; they then invented defensive scents for their Creatures.

"I grouped the Creatures into families based on shared scent defense mechanisms and had the students make a phylogenetic tree to show the relatedness of all of their Creatures. To teach about genetic survival, I caused a mass extinction of the Creatures, trashing their Organic City and leaving only two species behind. (Some students responded to this by saying that a meteor crashed into the landsite, while others proposed that a bacterial or viral outbreak was the culprit.) Students immediately built a second Never-Before-Seen Landsite for the surviving Creatures on another table, insisting that it be placed at the front of the classroom under their supervision.

This time, they were much more meticulous in meeting the requirements on my Criteria List to support living things. I had them build new Never-Before-Seen Creatures to inhabit the landsite with designs that incorporated the genetics of the surviving Creatures from the first landsite.

"On this new landsite, inhabited by species that were better adapted to survive, my students enthusiastically studied population ecology to learn how living things interact with each other and their environments. They researched the importance of the ability of living things to acquire energy in various ways to avoid a similar mass extinction event in the future. I found that teaching difficult topics—competition, mutualistic relationships, the carrying capacity of various environments, and how plants reproduce and acquire energy from the sun to provide nourishment on the cellular level—was a snap.

"Students are typically expected to just trust that these processes occur as we tell them. However, since I taught my students that their Creatures and landsite were analogs for what occurs in nature by having them build original models, they were better able to understand concepts in biology and to see the unseen."

Before Richard applied Design-Based Learning to teaching Science, few of his students went on to that field of study in college. By comparison, more than half of his Organic City students chose science-related fields.

GeoUnique Land (High School Geometry)

As a teacher in the Rowland Unified School District, Francisca Ortiz-Smith, who graduated from the master's degree program in 2007, developed a yearlong Design-Based Learning curriculum for her geometry classes with a student-built and student-run Never-Before-Seen tabletop City of the Future called GeoUnique Land. As students built

GeoUnique Land, Francisca taught them to identify its components as basic three-dimensional geometric objects through her Guided Lessons. She had them apply Math concepts, including measurements and formulas, to find perimeter, area, surface area, and volume. Her students enlarged and built a model of a map of GeoUnique Land using a coordinate plane; they divided the map, finding distance using the distance formula, Pythagorean Theorem, and Trigonometric ratios, and they studied properties of triangles. To live in GeoUnique Land, Francisca's students constructed Never-Before-Seen 3D Creatures/ Avatars, learning to identify their attributes to derive conditional statements, and they applied inductive and deductive reasoning to prove logic statements.

After building each object, students collected and interpreted data, analyzed results, and reflected on their own learning. Each of the 10 pathways in Francisca's yearlong curriculum consisted of one or more Design Challenges, depending on the scope of the objective being taught, "to engage students in the highest level skills of synthesis and assessment based on the 'Never-Before-Seen' concept," Francisca wrote in her master's project. "Through this concept, my students learned to develop and use criteria that resulted in the application of mathematical concepts.

"This was an excellent way to teach abstract geometric concepts and to provide students with ample opportunities to develop higher-level thinking skills." Francisca went on to refine her Design-Based Learning practice and involved all of the students in each of her Math classes in the building of one single City that remained in the center of the classroom as the context for every Math subject she taught.

Francisca Ortiz-Smith's students working in groups, studying different Math concepts to present to the whole class as a basis for revising their City.

Ugly as a Topic (Special Education, High School English)

Stephanie Na teaches AVID (Advancement Via Individual Determination, a college and career readiness elective), Advanced Composition, and Special Education English 2 at Workman High School in the Hacienda-La Puente Unified School District. In 2018, she described what happened when her Special Education English 2 Class students were building and governing a Starter City while reading *Ugly*, by Robert Hoge.

"If you've seen or heard of *Wonder*, the movie, then *Ugly* is a similar story of a boy who was born with severe facial deformities. Both protagonists go through massive facial reconstruction, bullying, and overcoming this adversity they were born with. As my students were building their Never-Before-Seen Starter City, I asked, 'Can you see a relationship between a Starter City and the book we're reading?' One student said, 'I think the relationship is that we are changing the structure of the City and it is similar to how the boy in the book had to have his face restructured.'

Francisca Ortiz-Smith's students working in groups, studying different Math concepts to present to the whole class as a basis for revising their City.

Students in Francisca Ortiz-Smith's Math classes surround their City as she teaches required Guided Lessons.

"That probably wouldn't be a mind-blowing response for teachers who teach general education students, but it was a huge connection/prediction for a student in a Special Day Class. There were other great answers as well, and I'm looking forward to continuing to build that bridge or 'hug' as we like to call it. Design-Based Learning is definitely more of a struggle with my Special Needs students, but when they make connections, it's more than worth it.

"Design-Based Learning has not only changed my teaching and who I am as a teacher, but has changed me into a leader, because I'm able to see past what many people consider 'creative' to see that there are Never-Before-Seen solutions yet to be discovered. Design-Based Learning changed the way I think."

Stanford University (10th- to 12th-Grade Migrant Education Program)

Rigo Rodriguez, an Associate Professor of Chicano and Latino Studies at Cal State University, Long Beach, contacted me to describe his experience as a child with my Design-Based Learning methodology. In 1979, Rigo's older sister took part in a Design-Based Learning summer program at Stanford University and brought it home to share with the entire family. The four-year program at Stanford was funded by a special grant from the State of California for underserved high school students who were children of migrants.

I was hired to train trainers to spearhead the six-week, live-in summer program. By day, the students built and governed a small City in the classroom. By night, of their own volition, they transferred what they had learned about organization and leadership to shared decision-making in their dormitories. Many of those students who experienced Design-Based Learning in this way, and who had not been expected to excel, went on to significant academic success. Two of the students went to Harvard University; one went to MIT.

Here is what Rigo wrote:

Hello, Ms. Nelson.

I want to thank you for your innovative and creative use of the City in your methodology because it turned me into an urban planner. Allow me to explain . . .

My older sister, Hilda, participated as a high school junior in a summer program at Stanford University back in 1978 or 1979 for children of migrant workers based on your [work].

When Hilda came back from that summer program, she came back so enlightened. She had all of us (I'm the youngest of 13) build and run a small City in our home and make decisions as a family democratically. For migrant kids living in the isolated outskirts of the Salinas Valley, cities were such a mystery! That "second-hand smoke" experience led me to my career as an urban planner and my advocacy for Social Justice.

Anyway, to make a long story short, through my sister's influence I became curious about how cities are designed, how decisions are made in cities; so much so that I obtained a master's degree in urban planning (UC Irvine) and a doctorate in geography (USC). And now I teach at CSULB using cities as a framework for understanding policy development.

So, I'm contacting you to thank you for the trailblazing work you have done, which I'm sure has had so many positive ripple effects on people.

With much appreciation,

Rigo Rodriguez, PhD, M.U.R.P.
Associate Professor, Latina/o Public Policy
California State University, Long Beach
Board President, Santa Ana Unified School District

I invited Rigo to speak to the large group of attendees at the 14th year of the Design-Based Learning K–12 Summer Institute for Teachers at ArtCenter College of Design in Pasadena. He related how his parents and all 13 children built and "played" with a small City in their home and how the family used it to decide the allocation of their resources and even what movies to see as a family. There was not a dry eye in the room.

* * *

I am continually amazed to learn how far the influence of the methodology can spread and how engaging it can be for students of any age. Jessica Heim, a young teacher who completed her master's degree in Design-Based Learning at Cal Poly in 2016, sent me the following before she left classroom teaching in 2019 to hold the first Doreen Gehry Nelson Endowed Directorship of the UCLA Center X Design-Based Learning Project:

> Just a little love note to you about Design-Based Learning. I lost my 1st-grade spot when I resigned [due to a family tragedy] and when I was able to return, I got placed in 5th, which I never would have chosen. But even with 2/3 of my class being boys and many disengaged kids, I am in love and so happy with my older students. Not once have I had a behavior problem, and I attribute it to you and the Design-Based Learning methodology! They are so engaged and being super responsible with the committee jobs in the classroom and in the City we are starting to build. We did our Never-Before-Seen Creature Design Challenge today and they were lost in designing and building. The recess bell rang and a boy that last year didn't do his work and drove the teacher crazy (because he's so smart)

asked if I would let him stay in at recess to continue writing about his Creature! I sent a few students to the principal to share their designs and writing. She was so impressed that she took pictures and asked me to write a Design-Based Learning summary for her to post on our school website. I have a few teachers who want to do a monthly training because they see how happy I am teaching and how I have zero behavior problems and my students are so excited to learn!

—Jessica

IN THE VIRTUAL CLASSROOM

During the 2020–2021 Covid-19 pandemic, a pilot program through UCLA's Center X Design-Based Learning Project utilized my methodology for online teaching in K–12 classrooms. This successful program reimagined classroom practice and established a new platform for teacher training in the methodology that is applicable, too, in a hybrid environment in classrooms with a mix of students attending in person and virtually.

10th to 12th Grade (Science and History)

"Design-Based Learning makes virtual learning so much greater," said David Cameron, a Science and History teacher at Gabrielino High School in the San Gabriel Unified School District, and an authorized computer science Python teacher.

"My students learn Science and History online by doing all of these online Design Challenges. They work together 'behind the scenes' and really try to please each other and me. They tap into their creativity and interests to actively participate in the community we create.

"In organizing my online teaching, I tried to think of what was accessible for all students to create some form of manipulated three-dimensional space that would have a function they could explain to the class. For their individual City land parcels they could use a piece of cardboard or a piece of paper to build on. It didn't matter. Whatever they had around.

"To simplify building a City online, I have my students put a compass on the top of their piece of cardboard or 8½- × 11-inch piece of paper so that when I take an overhead picture for their slides, I know where north, south, east and west are. They build on their land parcels and then virtually position their individual parcels on the real city map so they can see what and who they are near, and what problems they will have as they redesign the real city as their City of the Future. I always ask, 'What problems do you see?' They can easily see, 'Oh, we don't have any transportation,' or I ask, 'How far apart are you?' and that gets them to look at the scale. They realize that things aren't within walking distance, that things aren't as close as they seem.

"By taking a closer look at a physical map of the area they are redesigning for the future, with only the roads left, they not only think about what will go where to decide what to build, they also consider what was once there. They say, 'Oh, that's why there's a dead-end there, because there used to be a railroad going through.'

"As we go along, I ask them, 'What else is our problem, and do we see any other solutions? What solutions have we learned about, and how could we make this different? What else could we add or do?' Sometimes they say, 'Oh, we messed this up,' or, 'We don't need this, we were overthinking.' I teach them to ask each other about their thought processes or how this might help, or why that might not work.

"To get them to create Never-Before-Seen solutions to Design Challenges, I say, 'Look, we already know solutions to problems that we've already had. What else might a solution look like?' Sometimes

I check in on students after 20 minutes in and say, 'We've seen that before, take it a step further. Do something different.'

"After I teach Guided Lessons about required subject matter, when I ask students to revise their designs based on what they have learned, some students want to and some do not, which is fine with me, because I can't control what materials they have in their house. When students say, 'I don't have a whole lot around me,' I ask them to think about the problem again and say what they would do if they had the materials.

"I think that more importantly, especially for virtual learning, it's just that they get to be heard. They know that they're being heard by their peers, and when they get into the Future City, they're all on the same map. Just because you know all about chemistry doesn't mean you're going to solve the problems of the City better than anyone else. So everyone feels that when they say, 'I built this to add to that,' there's a power in knowing that other students are looking at their slide showing what they built, and that they are being listened to as they explain what they did. I feel there's that sense of identity and fairness and freedom in just that simple interaction and in the fact that we're all trying to build stuff made of whatever we can find around and it doesn't have to be the most beautiful, but it's going to add something to our community.

"To teach my students to equitably solve the problems they identify in their City, I have both my History and Science students present their designs for the City and their problem-solving solutions in Town Hall meetings. We have a timekeeper, a secretary, and some other people who jump in and facilitate what's going to be talked about and for how long. Once they hit three points on the agenda for the meeting, we open it up for 5 to 10 minutes for discussion—we usually have a shared document that people can type suggestions on or they can say them out loud.

"To run the City, a Mayor is elected by the students. I assign Council Districts and Commissions—the latter are pretty much the same for both History and Science class (Protection is one commission; Commerce, Trade, Environment are some others), and after full class meetings, I have students move into breakout rooms, grouped according to whatever issues require Commission or District discussion. When students return to the full class, I have digital chat turned off so students will have to speak.

"Each class might have a slightly different way they want to do their meetings and they have the freedom to do it that way until I feel it's not working, and then I step in and say, 'We have to change this.'

"If participation is slow, I try to add an agenda item on my own to pique enough students' interest in putting their opinions down. I might say, 'We need a class song to play at the beginning of class,' because everyone has their opinion on music. I'll get 10 suggestions, and all of a sudden they're vested in the meeting and then we go to other agenda items.

"And, once or twice a week, I say, 'Take an hour, follow the Criteria List and build this part (whatever we're working on), then come back and show us.' We talk and they step away again and maybe revise if they need some more time and we talk again. By doing this, I get students to move away from the screen, to think about what we're doing away from the confines of the two-dimensional screen. I get more participation because they have something to talk about, since they all followed the Criteria List to build whatever they worked on.

"One of the more powerful things is getting every student to have a place on the map that the other students can see in a virtual environment. Yes, you can hide behind a box in the virtual classroom and just have your name there, and I can call on you and you can say something. But they can also look down at this public set of slides with their Creatures/Avatars on them, and maybe a building they made for the community, and then they feel a sense of belonging—that they are adding something to the community, whether virtually or not.

"There's this physical world that they are redesigning so they are definitely thinking in terms of community. And I'm constantly saying, 'Look at your neighborhood, look outside, let's get that feeling into our virtual classroom. How can you make that happen?' I try to reinforce that leap into how anything they build in three dimensions might look digitally and vice versa, and they start to see that connection. It's like we're dancing in both worlds in class.

"I've been trying to find a way my students can put their pieces together online. Some of them have started to render what the streets would look like with what the class has built, which is amazing. They've made it 3D and they've started putting it together. I didn't assign it. They just decided to do it. But if we can't quite stitch our City together, we still have to realize that we are in a shared place and our problems are the same, based on location. We still have to define our community virtually and that's very important.

"Recently, in one of my classes, I said, 'Let's get some more things for our City, let's get a logo, let's get some other things to make your online City and your class look great because I'm going to show your City to the other classes.' They started to come up with a logo and started to participate and encourage each other. With that freedom, all of a sudden, they were saying, 'Oh, I can do this.' They even wrote a song for their City. They put it all together, and said, 'This is our City now, this is what we're proud of most.' "

4th Grade

One November morning in 2020, Jessica Heim, UCLA's Center X Director of the Design-Based Learning Project, joined Roosevelt

Elementary School teacher Georgia Singleton's online class. Heim was observing the class as part of the Center X contract with the San Gabriel Unified School District to provide staff development in Design-Based Learning for K–12 teachers.

"When I entered Ms. Singleton's Zoom classroom," said Heim, "I was introduced to nearly 40 smiling 4th graders through my computer screen. Not one camera was turned off and all of the students seemed engaged and ready to learn. After Ms. Singleton greeted her students warmly, what she said next made me wish I were in the 4th grade again.

" 'Class, we have a message from our City's Avatars!' " she exclaimed. 'They are in the dark! You have learned about different types of energy. Please help! We need to decide together what kind of energy to have in our City so our Avatars can survive!'

"The students had been assuming leadership roles as Avatars for the City of the Future that they were collaboratively imagining and building online as the yearlong context for the subject matter Ms. Singleton was teaching them. For the past week, she had taught lessons about clean energy through various textbook readings, research, and videos about wind, solar, hydroelectric, geothermal, biomass, and tidal energy.

" 'Now that we've learned about clean energy,' Ms. Singleton told the class, 'we're going to meet in our Council Districts to determine what the best energy source for our City will be and to prepare for our Town Meeting.'

"(To promote higher-level thinking skills, creativity, collaboration, and communication, while still teaching the required grade-level content area standards, Ms. Singleton was connecting what she had taught her students back to the City they were building. At the same time, she was teaching the 4th graders how to establish and run a government for their City, by having her students role-play a government structure. Governance in a student-centered classroom is intrinsic to the Doreen Nelson Method of Design-Based Learning, promoting social responsibility, teaching concepts related to social justice and civics, and activating classroom management strategies and the division of labor among students.)

"Ms. Singleton instructed the students to go to breakout rooms representing each Council District, choose a leader, a recorder, and a timekeeper, discuss their research, then decide on their District's clean energy choice. When she asked if there were any questions, the students' interest and excitement were palpable. I was struck by how efficiently these 9- and 10-year-olds moved to their online breakout rooms and once there, how they were able to manage their time and stay on task. Student leaders called on their Council District members to share their ideas while a recorder wrote down each response and the timekeeper made sure that each student's voice was heard. The level of communication among the 4th graders was impressive. They listened to one another, asked meaningful questions, and justified their reasoning with facts and findings.

"After about 10 minutes in the breakout rooms, the whole class came back together and the Mayor called the Town Meeting to order. The Council District leaders took turns sharing their choices for the best energy source, citing their research. After every Council District presentation, a vote was taken and solar was the winning energy source for their City.

"At the end of class, I asked Ms. Singleton's students what they liked about meeting in Council Districts to discuss ideas and make decisions about their City. One shared that she 'felt happy because her voice was being heard.' Another student stated that she felt 'comfortable sharing.' One student shouted out, 'I've never felt better!'

"I asked what they liked about Design-Based Learning. 'I love using my imagination,' one student said. 'It's so fun.' "

10th to 12th Grade (Math)

"I started off the year completely overwhelmed," said Rana Masri, a Math teacher at Delmar High School, Model Continuation School for 10th–12th graders in the San Gabriel Unified School District.

"I had to prepare for four different classes and had my own two kids at home due to the Covid-19 shutdown, so I made the decision to not start Design-Based Learning right away. Instead, I began by running my Algebra class the standard way, with notes and guided practice. Of course, I had spent my summer learning an array of online tools to help make my online class more engaging, but when the year started, I was faced with black muted screens. All day. Every day. Students were isolated from each other and the world.

"I didn't last three weeks before I announced to my Math classes to start collecting household items like foil, paper, toilet paper rolls, cereal boxes, plastic utensils, etc."

After giving her students introductory Design Challenges that included building a Never-Before-Seen Creature/Avatar, Rana's third Design Challenge of the year was to have her students build a Never-Before-Seen Starter City as a place for their Avatars to live. Her goal was to create a more integrated classroom community through the use of the City, connect what her students built to the required Math curriculum, and at the same time address their social and emotional needs. "Unlike past years," Rana said, "students had to build their piece of the City at home. This was a big disadvantage. Students gain a lot of courage and creativity from being able to interact with their peers in person. But they didn't complain. Instead, they got straight to work."

Rana gave her students the following information:

Problem: It's the year 2030 and many creatures have been forced into isolation due to a pandemic.

Essential Question: How can we build a healthy community?

Design Challenge: Design a Never-Before-Seen Starter City.

"Building a City online was easier said than done," Rana said. "It was hard to figure out how to unify the City pieces that my students built on their individual land parcels at home. I had them take a top-down view of their land parcel, and on a Google slide had them paste their parcels on a gridded map of their City's real location. The 2D picture of their City of the Future that we compiled online was not as exciting as the in-person, 3D City from years past. But, it was better than not having a City, because with it, I was able to push my students to interact, talk, and communicate. To revise their Starter City, they had to discuss how to build to scale. I had them work together to calculate square footage and housing capacity. They were now using Math in a real-world capacity, solving problems, and interacting in an online setting.

"(When I asked them to come up with a name for their City, no one responded at first, so I gave them time to ponder and came back to it at the end of the period. At this point, many students unmuted themselves and shared the names they had come up with. We wrote down the list of names and voted on their favorite the next day. 'Mathlantis' was voted on by an overwhelming majority. The student who had suggested this name unmuted himself to say with much excitement, 'That's the name I suggested!' In this short activity, the students were able to voice their opinions and interact with one another, having fun in an online classroom.)

"The final Design Challenge for the trimester was for students to build a parabola in their City. The intention was to further revise the Starter City and add something of needed function. In addition, I wanted to take the abstract concept of quadratic functions and turn it into something real and tangible for them. They built their parabolas, gave them a Never-Before-Seen purpose, and placed them in the City. I then had them conduct a series of calculations to find the equation of the parabolas that they built.

"Often in a high school online classroom, when I would call on a student to participate, I would get a delayed response and sometimes no response at all. However, while conducting the parabola Design Challenge, students were quick to respond. When I checked in with them, they unmuted quickly and shared their calculations with me. I could tell that the students were all on task and engaged because they all completed their tasks and finished the assignment. Through this Design Challenge, my students demonstrated their understanding of the concept of quadratic functions and made comparisons to other algebraic concepts that they had learned throughout the year.

"I asked students how doing the parabola Design Challenge had impacted their understanding of the concept. One student responded, 'I feel like it was easier to work with the parabola that we built since we were measuring it in a real place.' Another student said, 'It helped me find the equation of a parabola and it made graphing easier. Design-Based Learning is also a nice break from notes and homework. Before the parabola Design Challenge, I didn't understand what axis of symmetry and vertex meant. After doing the Design Challenge and the calculations, I get it.' "

High School (English)

To prepare for teaching Design-Based Learning online, Kate Borihane, an English teacher in the Academic Design Program at Walnut High School in the Walnut Valley Unified School District, worked with a team of teachers: Jennifer Sorbara (Math), Emily Alder (U.S. History), Joshua Bandy (English), and Andrea Takahashi (World History).

"We met three or four times during the summer to adapt our curriculum," said Kate. "The first necessary step was to decide on how students would build their 3D artifacts from home without being in the classroom to work together on one landform and get a government up and running. We decided to have a supplies 'pick-up day' to provide students with materials that included a small piece of the larger landform they would be redesigning. We created grids representing larger landforms using Google Slides that students would continually reference as they planned and added their designs on a 2D Map of their 3D builds. In our planning sessions, we brainstormed tools that could potentially be used (Google Classroom, Tinkercad, Flipgrid, etc.) to apply Design-Based Learning via distance learning, as well as new procedures and guidelines for online collaboration and presentation. We created rubrics for student planning and communication. We discussed how to encourage maximum participation and interaction. We wanted students to be able to view each other's work, as they would be able to in a classroom. We decided to use the "Google Question" function on Google Classroom for video submissions. We came up with a plan that was functional with the hopes of returning to the classroom with an even better repertoire of tools, some of which we may even keep for certain Design Challenges going forward.

"When my online teaching began, I told my students they were going to build a Never-Before-Seen Domain that would be planned and built in a real-world geographic location that was devoid of human influence or infrastructure due to a natural disaster, essentially a blank slate. The first Design Challenge was to design a personal Avatar that represented their individual traits and personalities. The second Design Challenge was to build a Starter Domain.

"All of the steps in a Design Challenge, from introduction to collaboration and presentation, were completed online. I divided my second period sophomores into groups of four, each representing real geographic locations around the world. My students collaborated on Design Challenges in Google Meet breakout rooms that I monitored while they worked. In their groups, students filmed individual presentations and then sent their video clips to one group member to splice together before submitting to me on Google Classroom.

"I asked students to submit presentation videos in a way that would allow them to view each other's videos and to comment and give feedback online. This was done on Google Classroom by assigning a "Google Question" instead of "Google Assignment" for the video submissions. I checked a small box that allowed students to 'reply' to one another. Since one group member consistently posted the video, the other group members had to submit a one-word response, such as 'finished,' in order to view the other groups' videos. This worked well and they were then able to provide structured feedback, based on guidelines I provided. This process simulated viewing live presentations in class.

"I found that students really need the teacher to be present, not only to monitor them, but to encourage their creativity by asking them to explain their ideas during the planning process and after giving presentations. This meant jumping into individual breakout rooms one at a time while students planned and built. I made time to reflect with students before beginning Guided Lessons about the successes and failures of the Design Challenge they had finished. Getting their feedback involved time for breakout rooms, so that I could review with students and they could ask questions about their performance and assessment. Students, I found, needed to talk it through and appreciated the time to reflect with me and with their groups. They seemed more communicative and asked more specific questions than they would have during whole group discussions or even in emailed communications.

"Unsurprisingly, monitoring group work and communicating to students without physical proximity was challenging. Here's what did surprise me: My students built creatively and had wonderful Never-Before-Seen ideas, despite the lack of a physical classroom environment."

2nd Grade

"I teach in the San Gabriel Unified School District and my small class, which includes several kids with special needs, is quite diverse in terms of demographics and learning styles," said Daphne Chase, a 2nd-grade teacher at Wilson Elementary School. "My grade level teaching objectives during COVID were the same as pre-COVID, even though some of the tools in the virtual world are a little different. I wanted my virtual classroom to have some similarity to what Design-Based Learning promotes in person. Building a City gives students a land of 'make believe,' that makes them want to talk to each other and think critically and creatively, giving me a way in to teaching the lessons I need to teach. When my students present their Never-Before-Seen designs in person, you can see all of this discussion and engagement. This is what I wanted to recreate virtually, but when I started teaching online, I couldn't get all of my students to participate in Design Challenges and I couldn't get them to talk.

"(There were also some minor problems: some parents couldn't resist solving and building the Design Challenge for their child. I get that. I'm also a parent, and it's hard to watch your kids struggle, but as a teacher, I know how important that struggle is for students to really grow. Other family members, not realizing what students were trying to accomplish by building on a piece cardboard, threw out what they had built, thinking it was trash; one brother was not happy that his sister was getting to build stuff, and crumpled up her work.)

"I found the breakout rooms to be the answer to getting my students to engage in discussions about the City they were building online. It was terrifying at first, but the power of the breakout rooms is undeniable. It was important to make sure the students had a goal, a leader, and screen-sharing ability. By framing these breakout sessions as 'District Meetings,' I was able to get more students to participate in the Design Challenges because they would hold each other accountable. Kids would say, 'Hey, you're in this district, what are we missing? How can you help our district?' They were able to revise their designs, and at the same time, help someone who hadn't started building. This was really powerful.

"Organizing breakout rooms and making sure that students have set government roles and something to do there is crucial to making them feel accountable and less inclined to be disruptive. (One of the most important roles is the recorder, who writes down what they find in the chat box. A lot of kids, especially the shy ones, are more willing to offer their ideas in chat.) I kept two computers running in order to be present in 'stealth mode' in at least two breakout rooms at any time to see and hear what they were doing, keeping my camera off and remaining a passive element in the students' discussions. And, keeping the breakout sessions short gave students a sense of urgency to complete the work, without my having to control the conversations as I went from small group to whole group lessons.

"To have my students begin building their City online, I started with a map of San Gabriel. I had them go into Google Maps, find our school and notice there is a beautiful reservoir, an ideal water source, close to the school. Once the location was clear to them, I mailed each student a land parcel that was their piece of the total area they were going to redesign. The parcel each student received was randomized, but correlated to one of the grids I had drawn on the map of the area. Once students got their land parcel, we discussed the grid coordinates each of them had received. In this way, I was organically teaching about maps, even before the Design Challenge began.

"After they located their land parcels on the map, I put my students in three Council Districts and assigned matching breakout rooms. Setting up the groups was vital to get the kids talking and working together about proposals for their City. These districts gave students a way to function as communities within a community.

"To give my students clarity about how the City would come together as a whole, I had them take photos of their land parcels from a bird's-eye view. I then resized their photos to fit within the map. When compared with a City built in the classroom, this wasn't ideal, but there were some advantages to being able to envision the whole City in this way. It got students curious and talking. They said, 'I can see my piece there,' or, 'Oh, who's that next to me?' Even when a student's photo was not of good quality, it didn't really matter. I put it in the City to give others an idea of the whole. (I also asked the kids to take a photo from a side view to see what their buildings looked like in 3D.)

"When I paired Design-Based Learning with online tools like Google Slides, Jamboard, or Seesaw, I was able to promote the inter-activity at the heart of the methodology. It was important to set up criteria for using online platforms, because things can go awry rather quickly. Kids have the ability to delete aspects that they have not built, they can delete an entire slide, and they can scribble over somebody's things. Overall, this planning paid off. We even had a class meeting to talk about how fun it was to use online platforms and about making sure that nobody's feelings got hurt and that everybody's ideas got shared. This launched conversations about respect and responsibility. (Seesaw also stores some history of what students build.)

"One of the main challenges I faced in the implementation of Design-Based Learning in the online classroom was how hard it was for kids to look for problems within their City. A difference between online and in-person classrooms is how in person, kids see clearly, 'Oh, there's a problem here. This is what we need to do next.' They have a little more difficulty finding those problems online. To solve this issue, I started with a discussion about pathways for movement in the City and had students decide what each of their pathways represented in the context of the City. Were specific pathways built for carriers, just for private use, were they natural pathways or synthetic? Again, the goal was to get kids really talking, collaborating, and thinking about these problems. To teach the use of descriptive vocabulary and persuasive language, I had them draft a real estate flyer to describe their Never-Before-Seen Shelters, decide on prices, and figure out how to contact buyers. All of the ways that kids show their knowledge in Design-Based Learning were on full display in this online activity. The idea isn't *what* they build, it is *why* they build it and what they're imagining and learning in the process.

"What I found in teaching Design-Based Learning online for the first time was that everything took longer than I thought it would. I had to give students more time to complete Design Challenges, explain my Criteria List more slowly, and devote more time to answering questions. If I continue teaching online, I will present and explain the Design Challenge before a break, to give my students time to think about it. I might even share the Criteria List on my screen during lunch to give them more time to prepare for what they will build. The build itself doesn't take that long, but the power behind having that build is worth every minute."

Kindergarten (Private School)

Natalie Bezdjian, a kindergarten teacher at the Rose and Alex Pilibos Armenian School in Hollywood, California, and a Design-Based Learning teacher trainer, was daunted at first at the thought of teaching kindergarten online. "I was concerned about my students' attention span, participation, and behavior," she said. "On their first day of online learning, I told them they would be building a Never-Before-Seen

Creature. (I had previously emailed their parents regarding the recycled materials students would need to collect for their online Design Challenges.)

"To introduce my students to the concept of Never-Before-Seen, I displayed pictures of weird animals that included a duck with a banana torso. Then I had my students share and discuss the different kinds of recycled items they had collected. They were yelling out of turn, showing what they had on the screen. It was happy chaos. I was surprised by the enthusiasm they displayed and it gave me the courage to continue. To teach Math standards, I had them describe the attributes—shapes, size, color, texture, etc.—of their recycled materials.

"Once my students 'played' with these recycled items they were ready to build Never-Before-Seen Creatures by learning to follow my Criteria List that included English standards: 'Introduce the Creatures' Names (Noun)' and 'Show the Never-Before-Seen Creatures' Abilities (Action Verb).' Once students built their Creatures, they presented them to the class.

"When they encountered problems, I created a 'Problem List' and called a five-minute online classroom meeting. I had them take turns by raising their hands and unmuting to share their concerns about their Never-Before-Seen Creatures. All of their concerns related to themes in the subjects that I was planning to teach. For example, their Never-Before-Seen Creatures needed shelter, food, friends, a school, a hospital, cars, money, clothes, etc. Finally, my students felt their Creatures needed a place to be together. The time had come for them to build and name their Never-Before-Seen City of the Future.

"Once they started building their City online on their individual land parcels (cardboard or paper), I organized students into government committees (Communication, Beautification, Energy, and Record Keeping). For example, students in the Record Keeping Committee took attendance by looking at the screen and counting how many students were present. The Communication Committee repeated the directions for students who had questions. This prepared my students to learn about governance and social responsibility as their City grew.

"I've been building Cities in the classroom with my students for nine years and each year, as my comfort level with the methodology grew, I found more ways to be creative in my planning. I was relieved to discover that I could apply the methodology to design my online teaching, too."

7th and 8th Grade (Private School)

"I did virtual Design-Based-Learning last March to June in 2020, and although I have been in the classroom from late that September till now, I still have half a dozen virtual students that I teach simultaneously with the students in my classroom," said Jeanne Miller, who teaches 7th- and 8th-grade honors-prep English Language Arts, Social Studies, Ancient Church History, and Family Life at St. Bonaventure, a Catholic school in Orange County, California.

"My virtual students participate in the Design Challenges and present their work. Because audio can be so unsteady, I always offer them the choice of writing their presentations for us nonvirtuals to read or for someone else to read aloud, but without fail, every one of them prefers to present their work themselves. That is true pride of ownership, which is a trait that many students don't seem to have any more with the advent of computers. My virtual students collect their own happy trash, and they drop their creations off at the school office so I can add them to our 3D Community."

* * *

The term "City Building Education" was coined in the early 1970s at the Smithsonian Institution in Washington, DC. It referred to the physical aspects of urban living and the invisible fabric of social, political, and economic relationships that require creative thinking. I liked that, and I initially called my methodology "City Building Education." I later found that term inhibited my ability to explain the purpose of having students build and govern a City in the classroom. I needed a term that would make it clear that the methodology is not about architecture, urban planning, or arts and crafts, but instead, a relatively small, student-built City is a visible tool for stimulating creative thinking, bringing subject matter to life, and making learning stick and become reusable.

Teachers continue to discover the cross-curricular versatility of building an original, three-dimensional, tabletop City based on a real location—in the physical classroom and in the virtual classroom—and how it serves as a stage for creative thinking. (Those who develop only a two-dimensional version of a City, don't base it in a real location, or make the City too small, find subsequent student interest and achievement results less significant.) I have concluded that all human artifacts and thought can be examined through the lens of a city, a civilization, a culture, or a system. Art, Math, Science, Literature—every subject in the curriculum is associated with human development. The city itself is an original human design.

THE METHODOLOGY

"Please don't make me go out on the playground and drag my wagon around pretending I'm a pioneer moving West, it's humiliating." My 5th-grade student Michael was adamant, refusing to join his fellow students on an imagined trek Westward to see if the covered wagons they had built would make it across rugged terrain. I thought he was just being a smart aleck, because he had said that he liked finding out about the ratio between the front and rear wheels of his wagon, how the front wheels turned with a movable axle, and why the bowed wagon top was covered with Osnaburg fabric (all part of the 5th-grade curriculum).

I was trained to be a teacher at the UCLA Lab School by John Dewey's disciples, so whether the context for learning was Native cultures, the Pilgrims, the pioneers, foreign cultures, or the United Nations, I had my students do research and then make artifacts or models to display what they learned and then role-play in the setting.

At the start of the school year, I would bring in objects that represented the subject matter (**BIG TOPICS**) that I needed to teach: "Realia." I went to the Natural History Museum and rented artifacts that the pioneers used to sustain life, everything from a wagon wheel and a sluice box to costumes. I went into the Japanese community and got loans of kimonos, chopsticks, getah, and tatami mats. When using literature to teach about courage, I plastered photos of heroic acts across the classroom walls.

My next step was to have the students replicate something that they had learned about and use what they made for "play." Armed with their replicas, they pretended to be living in a house in Japan with shoji screens, pioneers going West, or courageous heroes.

In Michael's class, my students learning about the Westward Movement imagined that they were the pioneers. As part of their study, I had them build covered wagons (the size of a shoe box), take their wagons to the playground, and "drag" them from Independence, Missouri (which I drew on the playground with chalk), to California, over mountains and rivers that I made of books and rocks covered with construction paper. All of my students, except for Michael, seemed to be relieved that they were out of their chairs and having fun.

Long after I developed my teaching methodology, I figured out what was bothering me about Michael's reluctance to "play."

Watching iconic American designers Frank Gehry, my brother, and Ray and Charles Eames "play" with their models, I concluded that Michael had been right. As Frank designed his original buildings, and as Ray and Charles designed their unique furniture, films, and exhibitions, they "messed" with their inventions endlessly. Their designs began as a response to a challenge; the resulting products were realized when these creative people experimented with their imagined designs and refined them through research.

Had I asked Michael to imagine designing his covered wagon with the same constraints imposed in the 1800s—no electricity, the need to navigate various landscapes and provide families with shelter from the elements—he would have learned about methods of mobility and protection, and he most certainly would have wanted to test out his design. Instead, I had asked my students to replicate an artifact to underscore what I had taught them about the perils of the Westward Movement.

Most of the learning in my classroom back then was focused on the transmission of information to my students from me, and from textbooks and other resources. I was not fostering my students' ability to think creatively and to express themselves. Indeed, asking students to replicate what already exists can leave them with the impression that only people in books are creative and inventive. Merely replicating something that someone else has accomplished inadvertently stifles self-expression. Yet at the beginning of my teaching career, applying John Dewey's pedagogy, all my hands-on projects had students build models of what I showed them. I had fun and my students were learning the required information, but it stopped there. I discovered that there is a profound disconnect between having students replicate subject matter by building physical objects and what I wanted my students to achieve: the higher-level thinking skills for original thought and creativity, as described in Benjamin Bloom's 1956 *Taxonomy of Educational Objectives*—a classification system defining levels of cognition.

The answer to my quandary came when I pictured Bloom's *Taxonomy* as a "Learning Ladder." I imagined turning this "Ladder" around so that the last step described in the *Taxonomy*, creativity and self-expression, started the learning process. Teaching "backwards" this way enabled me to pre-assess what students already knew about subject matter and piqued their curiosity about what I would be teaching them.

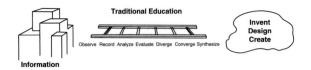

TEACHING/LEARNING LADDERS
(High-Level Thinking Skills)–a comparison

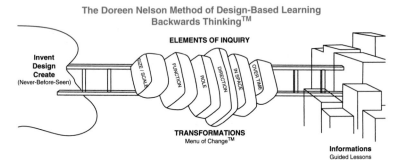

Long-Range Plan: Sample Sequence of Never-Before-Seen (NBS) Design Challenges

NBS Starter City	NBS Creature	NBS Shelter	NBS Government (Division of Labor)	NBS Place to Shop	NBS Way to Move People & Goods	NBS Places to Learn	NBS Revised Starter City

The Learning Ladder graphic illustrates how teaching for creative thinking through my method of Design-Based Learning with Backwards Thinking™ achieves all of the higher-level thinking skills listed in Benjamin Bloom's *Taxonomy*. At the top of the graphic, I depict Bloom's *Taxonomy* as a "Traditional Education" ladder that begins with the teacher's delivery of information and leads, ideally, to students acquiring those higher-level thinking skills deemed necessary for invention, creation, and design.

In my early career as a classroom teacher, I spent all my time imparting information, but teaching students how to meaningfully assimilate it was another story (as evidenced by my student Michael and his covered wagon). I never reached the final goal of the *Taxonomy*: having students invent, create, or design original artifacts based on what I had taught them. I wasn't alone. Other teachers felt—and feel—this way. My depiction of the "Traditional Education" ladder represents this common disconnect between teaching information and teaching for self-expression.

The Doreen Nelson Method of Design-Based Learning, Backwards Thinking™ Learning Ladder reverses the first and last steps that Bloom described. It begins with "Invent, Create, Design," as students respond to **BIG TOPIC** Design Challenges by roughly building 3D artifacts to represent their initial thinking about subject matter before they crack open a textbook. Through learned information acquired during a teacher's required Guided Lessons, students delve deeper into that subject matter to revise their original 3D designs and place them in the context of a City of the Future, or a Never-Before-Seen Community, Settlement/Colony, Ancient Civilization, Biome, Biosphere, Business, or any other curriculum-based setting that changes as it is built and governed.

Creating artifacts for a remote future and learning how to revise them invites students to speculate about "what if" and practice how one thing might become something else and why. "TRANSFORMATIONS, Menu of Change™" on my Learning Ladder, guides students to practice what John Dewey called "experimental inquiry," a thought process he described as being "very near the attitude of the scientific mind." Shown here is a sample vocabulary for ways students can try out making deliberate change when they get stuck coming up with original ideas. For example, a student builds a Never-Before-Seen Shelter for their Starter City of the Future, but it is too big or too small (Size/Scale), and how the Shelter will work for the inhabitant has not been thought out (Function).

Built into each Design Challenge, the words on the Menu of Change™ prompt students to think critically about concepts they must adhere to in applying subject matter to revise their Never-Before-Seen artifacts in order to have them work in the context of their City of the Future. The teacher-led questioning about the Size, Scale, Function, etc., of the students' artifacts targets the higher-level thinking skills in the *Taxonomy* that lead to transfer of learning (Non-Specific Transfer of Learning). Giving students vocabulary for ways to experiment with changing one thing into something else in varied academic and daily life settings activates their conscious understanding of how to use and reuse information. This is metacognition.

I gathered this vocabulary while researching Non-Specific Transfer of Learning, wanting students to know that they were capable of changing something that exists (for example: clothing, housing, cars, the way we shop, the way we communicate, school, energy sources, and waste disposal) into something original as a response to a need or problem—or just for fun. I wanted them to internalize the fact that change can be deliberate and doesn't have to be an accident or a twist of fate, and that the kinds of changes they would learn to make would apply in a variety of settings. I verified that when such great thinkers as scientist Jonas Salk, landscape architect Lawrence Halprin, artist Claes Oldenburg, electronic composer Morton Subotnick, and my brother, architect Frank Gehry, brought their innovations into being, they solved problems through seemingly automatic, observational experimentation that the words I named represent. As part of my research, I later had the good fortune to formalize this vocabulary through conversations with Salk, Alan Kay, and others.

When I first taught "backwards," presenting the "TRANSFORMATIONS, Menu of Change™" concepts (Size/Scale, Function, Role, Direction, In Space, Over Time) as my students imagined and built their tabletop, Never-Before-Seen Starter City of the Future, I discovered that their ability to apply and reuse what they learned (Non-Specific Transfer of Learning) happened seemingly automatically.

By exercising "Experimental Inquiry" through the higher-level thinking skills named by Bloom (as shown on my Learning Ladder), my students learned to observe, analyze, record, and evaluate in preparation for making revisions to the artifacts that they built to represent their initial thinking about subject matter topics.

During the course of my research in K–12 classrooms that resulted in my methodology, I learned that when requiring students to use their imagination to be creative and launch their "experimental inquiry," words matter. A "Never-Before-Seen Shelter" results in an original artifact as opposed to a "house." A "Never-Before-Seen Creature" results in an original artifact as opposed to an "animal." A "Never-Before-Seen City of the Future" avoids the replication of a "city" that exists today. (Again, the same holds true if the Never-Before-Seen City of the Future is a Never-Before-Seen Community, Settlement/Colony, Ancient Civilization, Biome, Biosphere, Business, or any other curriculum-based setting.)

One way to think about my methodology is that ultimately everything can be a design problem: what to wear to a Halloween party if you don't have a costume, what the picnic table is going to look like for the 4th of July, what citizens can do to save the planet from global warming.

As the "client," the teacher invites students to become the designers of their City of the Future. The kicker is that students role-play governing their City as they build it. By role-playing, and through back-and-forth discussions to reach agreement on rules and regulations, they learn to take on social responsibility and make decisions about social justice in order to make changes to revise their Starter City.

The "Long-Range Plan: Sample Sequence of Never-Before-Seen (NBS) Design Challenges" shown on the Learning Ladder graphic represents a progression of Design Challenges taking place over a semester or school year.

In K–12 Design-Based Learning classrooms—physical or virtual—learning *always* starts with the spatial domain, because tactile learning sticks in the brain and increases focus and retention. On individual pieces of a predetermined landform representing a real location or system, students roughly build a tabletop Starter City of the Future, or other Never-Before-Seen contextual, built environment, based on required curriculum. *The interdependence of the parts of the City is a metaphor for the interconnectedness of all subject matter.*

Design Challenges are derived from **BIG TOPICS** in any K–12 curriculum. Each Design Challenge is posed to students to elicit their initial thinking about subject matter and Essential Questions by having them build Never-Before-Seen artifacts for their City, prior to being taught required Guided Lessons (**small topics**).

Students build Never-Before-Seen Creatures/Avatars to be their surrogates as "citizens" of the City. They build Never-Before-Seen Places and Spaces to revise and grow their Starter City. Having students build on their individual land parcels and bring them together—as parts to a contextual whole—to determine how their City will function, teaches students to seek out the problems they will solve in a series of progressively more complex Design Challenges.

If the teacher's City "story" is about a Never-Before-Seen Community, Settlement, or Civilization, for example, the "built-in" dilemmas that students invariably identify and solve as Design Challenges could include not enough places for others to live (**BIG TOPIC: SHELTER**), not enough ways to get around the City, pathways that lead nowhere or directly into someone's front door (**BIG TOPIC: MOVEMENT**), too many places for shopping (**BIG TOPIC: EXCHANGE**), and not enough for education, health services, recreation, outdoor spaces, and other necessities for daily living (**BIG TOPIC: WELL-BEING**).

(See Chapter 2 for teacher stories using the methodology across grade levels and subject areas. These include high school Science teacher Richard Rosa's "Organic City: Seeing the Unseen," built by students to learn about evolution and the survival of living things.)

After gaining real-world information through Guided Lessons, reading textbooks, and doing research, students revisit their initial thinking about the subject matter presented during a Design Challenge, compare their built solutions to what they have learned, and revise their solutions by discussing the changes they would make and/or by physically modifying their designs. A teacher's semester- or year-long City "story" evolves with each dilemma that students identify and solve by building and refining their Never-Before-Seen answers to Design Challenges. At the same time, students practice civic activism and responsibility as they learn to assume roles in their City government and experience the social give-and-take of working together for a common goal: a functional City made whole by a diversity of imagined possibilities.

Regardless of a student's age, by starting with building before textbook study, the playfulness inherent in my method of Design-Based Learning seals the deal.

TAPPING INTO TEACHERS' INNATE CREATIVITY

Teachers learn the methodology in a similar hands-on way in trainings by graphically visualizing an integrated curriculum. They learn a dynamic way of planning by making and manipulating physical informational tools that they can use, reuse, and reconfigure according to their grade level or subject matter requirements for a semester or school year. They learn to make long-range plans in three steps, using the tactile, visual, and written domains to ensure deep understanding of how an integrated curriculum functions in a Design-Based Learning classroom. When K–12 teachers learn to apply the methodology to their regular curriculum and make a comprehensive, semester- or year-long plan, they are often surprised to find, as they dig into the state standards to develop the lessons they need to teach, that students' creative and higher-level thinking skills are consistently required.

Teacher trainings begin two-dimensionally, with a study of the Design-Based Learning methodology's 6½ Steps of Backwards Thinking™. The trainings continue with the creation of a simple, three-dimensional planning tool: 3D Red Triangles that represent the relationship between a **BIG TOPIC** (the subject of a Design Challenge) and **small topics** (a teacher's required Guided Lessons). During the trainings, the Design Challenges and Guided Lessons, brainstormed using the 3D Red Triangles, are refined and written on 2D Curriculum Integration Charts. The information on the Curriculum Integration Charts is further refined as teachers create their individual 3D Long-Range Planning Boards, each displaying a monthly, **BIG TOPIC** Design Challenge and its related **small topics** (Guided Lessons). The information displayed on the Long-Range Planning Boards is easily modified to accommodate changes in grade levels, subject matter, and curricular requirements. (Teacher trainings range from a 40-hour immersive introduction to a variety of options that provide up to 120 additional hours of follow-up and support as teachers apply the methodology in their classrooms.)

The physicality of the Design-Based Learning planning process, taught in three different ways, brings out teachers' innate creativity. Their planning for tomorrow and beyond becomes personal. When they walk into the classroom, they can't wait to see it at work. ("Once it connected it was just like butter," said educator Terry Ceja. "One idea trickled into another and pretty soon I couldn't sleep because I was so excited! I discovered I have imagination and creativity, and I use it in everything I do now.")

THE 6½ STEPS OF BACKWARDS THINKING™

K–12 classroom teachers find that Backwards Thinking™, the method of Design-Based Learning, doesn't require a whole new series of lessons or a new curriculum. All that is needed is to rethink the sequence of lessons to amplify any mandated curriculum and "sneak up" on learning: as students express their ideas by roughly building a tabletop City with original 3D artifacts, what seems like fun to them, in reality, leads them to engage with the required Guided Lessons that follow.

During my visit with respected education expert Jerome Bruner in 2015, he said, "I worry that today's drive toward subject matter accountability is freezing creative thinking." My years of experience have shown me that it is not an either/or, that good test scores and creative thinking are compatible. The data I have collected consistently show that students in classrooms using the Design-Based Learning methodology excel. The quantitative data show that standardized test scores in Language Arts, Math, Science, and other subjects improve markedly, even for English language learners and those with learning disabilities. The qualitative data collected from students, teachers, administrators, and parents through surveys and anecdotal records describe the positive impact of Design-Based Learning on student engagement and understanding.

Design-Based Learning, with its 6½-step process of Backwards Thinking™, has the same learning goals as traditional methodologies. It begins with **BIG TOPIC** Design Challenges that open the door to students' creativity by asking them to build artifacts to represent their own ideas about **BIG TOPIC** subject matter. High-level learning begins immediately.

Having students use the vocabulary for **BIG TOPICS** as they build their solutions to Design Challenges within the context of their City or other built environment, provides practice in the higher-level thinking skills that make learned information reusable (Non-Specific Transfer of Learning). During this process, Design Challenges always adhere to the vocabulary for the Guided Lessons that are taught after students build and evaluate their original, City-related artifacts according to a teacher's pre-set Criteria List. Asking for "houses" simply gets houses. Asking for "roads" gets ordinary roads. Students' creative thinking skyrockets when Design Challenges are named as **BIG TOPICS** that define the function of what their designs are meant to accomplish. Teachers ask students to build Never-Before-Seen Living Creatures (not "animals"), Never-Before-Seen Shelters or Ways of Protection (not "houses" or "jails"), Never-Before-Seen Places of Learning (not "schools"), Never-Before Seen Places to Exchange Goods or Information (not "malls" or "the internet"), Never-Before Seen Pathways and Carriers (not "roads," "freeways," "bike paths," "trucks," or "trains").

Following each Design Challenge, students compare what they built according to their initial ideas to new information acquired during the study that follows. Textbooks, other source materials, and technology become resources to support students' creative and critical thinking as they are taught required subject matter Guided Lessons. With new information, students revise their built artifacts by talking or writing about them or rebuilding them.

The more that teachers ask students to give physical shape to their thinking about **BIG TOPIC** subject matter before Guided Lessons, and the more they prompt students to identify and solve problems within the context of a built City by demanding originality, the deeper their students' thinking becomes.

To facilitate teachers' understanding of the Backwards Thinking™ process, Leslie Stoltz, a teacher at Chaparral Middle School in the Walnut Valley Unified School District in Diamond Bar, California, who trained hundreds of teachers in the methodology, worked with me to develop the 6½ Steps of Backwards Thinking™ circle chart guide.

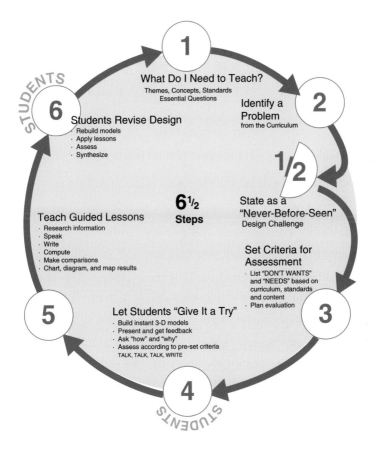

**The Doreen Nelson Method of Design-Based Learning
Backwards Thinking Process**

Backwards Thinking™

Step 1: What Do I Need to Teach? BIG TOPICS, Themes, Concepts, Standards

Each Design Challenge is derived from an Essential Question organized around a **BIG TOPIC** that comes from the required standards. Examples: **PROTECTION, TRADE, MIGRATION.**

Step 2: Identify a "Problem" from the Curriculum

Examples: Why do people need protection, to trade, or to migrate? How do natural resources define cultures? Why did cities come into being?

Step 2½: State a "Never-Before-Seen" Design Challenge

Calling a Design Challenge "Never-Before-Seen" asks for original thinking, not replication.

Step 3: Set Criteria for Assessment

A Criteria List establishes the requirements for successfully completing a Design Challenge. A Criteria List with points for evaluation is the reference tool for each Design Challenge, a kind of teacher surrogate, that teaches students to self-assess.

- List **"DON'T WANTS"** and **"NEEDS"** based on curriculum, standards, and content
- Plan evaluation

Step 4: Let Students "Give It a Try" (Duration of each Design Challenge: 45 minutes to two hours)

Students:

- Build instant 3D models (Never-Before-Seen artifacts)
- Present and get feedback
- Learn to ask "how" and "why"
- Learn to self-assess according to pre-set criteria

TALK, TALK, TALK, WRITE: Students learn to describe their designs through presentation and repeated discussion as preparation for writing.

Step 5: Teach Guided Lessons—Small Topics (Duration: one week to four weeks)

Teach Guided Lessons in subjects specifically related to a Design Challenge, constantly making the connection to students' Never-Before-Seen artifacts to amplify their understanding of subject matter.

Examples: the mathematics of the student-built artifact's size, shape, and volume; its scientific feasibility, the language art skills of reading, speaking, writing.

Students:

- Research information
- Speak
- Write
- Compute
- Make comparisons
- Chart, diagram, and map results

Step 6: Have Students Revise Designs

By describing changes to their artifacts, students engage in higher-level thinking. Having students rebuild their artifacts promotes accountability by making their learning of Guided Lessons visible.

Students:

- Rebuild 3D Models
- Apply Guided Lessons
- Assess
- Synthesize

Design Challenge to build a Never-Before-Seen Creature Shelter, taught as an integrated curriculum at the 3rd-grade level.

Step 1: What Do I Need to Teach?

The **BIG TOPIC** is **PROTECTION**.

The Essential Question: How do humans protect themselves and their world?

Step 2: Identify The Problem

Students' Never-Before-Seen Creatures/Avatars (built in a previous Design Challenge) need a way to protect themselves from the elements and enemies in their City.

Step 2½: State the BIG TOPIC Design Challenge

Build a Never-Before-Seen Shelter for your Creature/Avatar. ("Our creatures need to protect themselves. Invent how they will do it in a Never-Before-Seen Shelter that you build." To promote originality, the teacher emphasizes, "your designs need to be something that you have never seen before.")

Step 3: Set Criteria for Assessment

Introduce the Criteria List for the Never-Before-Seen Creature Shelter Design Challenge. The words on the Criteria List come from the Social Studies and Science curricula that require the teaching of how humans have protected themselves from extremes of nature and other dangers. This vocabulary pre-pares students for the Guided Lessons ahead. The **DON'T WANTS** for the students' Never-Before-Seen Shelters are written on the left side of the Criteria List in red, meaning "stop" or "no," prompting students to air their opinions about what they should avoid as they design their Never-Before-Seen artifacts and why. The **NEEDS** on the right are written in green, meaning "yes" or "go," adhering to curricular requirements. Check for understanding of the words on the Criteria List by having students read the list and ask questions for clarification.

CRITERIA LIST FOR A NEVER-BEFORE-SEEN CREATURE SHELTER		
Don't Wants	**Needs**	**Points**
Already Seen	Never-Before-Seen	5
Drawings	3D	5
Ordinary houses with the usual doors and windows	Ways to get in and out	10
	Ways to provide light and air	10
Temporary solutions	Forever solutions for protection from the extremes of nature: Rain Floods Wind Hurricanes Extreme heat and cold Earthquakes	10
Harmful or ugly solutions: guns, bars on the shelters, or prisons	Protection from enemies	10

Step 4: Let Students Give It a Try

Duration: 45 minutes to two hours

Materials: Paper, recycled materials, Criteria List

Working alone or in groups, after selecting a variety of materials, students have a minimum of 30 minutes to build their solutions to the Never-Before-Seen Shelter Design Challenge, adhering to the Criteria List. If they start building forts or houses, referring them back to the Criteria List stops replication. After building their rough artifacts (which they will revise as they learn more), students learn to give oral presentations explaining their reasoning for their Never-Before-Seen Shelters. They learn to listen and to question their classmates' presentations. They Talk, Talk, Talk, Write. If working in small groups, students vote on the best design in their group; each group presents a summary of its chosen design to the whole class. Students then draw and write about the details of their Never-Before-Seen Shelters.

Step 5: Teach the Guided Lessons—Small Topics (Duration: one week to a month)

Students are guided to:

- Collect and compare scientific data to their Never-Before-Seen Creature Shelter solutions for weather events and earthquakes.
- Determine the geometric shapes and volume of their artifacts.
- Diagram their Never-Before-Seen Shelters, labeled with exact measurements.
- Differentiate how humans throughout history have protected themselves.
- Write and edit original compositions using descriptive language to explain what it's like to live in their Never-Before-Seen Shelters.

Step 6: Have Students Revise Their Designs

Students apply the information learned through Guided Lessons to revise their designs. They propose and discuss the changes they want to make to their Never-Before-Seen Creature Shelters and why. The revision process is based on students' research and the changes they propose making to their artifacts. Their proposed revisions can be spoken or built. Built is better.

KICK-STARTING THE MAKING OF AN INTEGRATED CURRICULUM

During their in-depth training in the methodology, K–12 teachers learn to make a semester or yearlong plan through a series of hands-on experiences to ensure understanding of how to create an integrated curriculum. They craft 3D Red Triangles, write Curriculum Integration Charts (2D), and fabricate Long-Range Planning Boards (2D and 3D). The Long-Range Planning Boards reflect each teacher's unique, integrated curriculum in a comprehensive, creative, and highly professional display. This physical planning process gives form to a contextual "story" that evolves over time, capturing the imagination of students as they learn to seek and solve problems by building a sequence of three-dimensional artifacts for their City to represent their thinking about what they are learning.

Over the 50-plus years that I have guided teachers through this process, invariably when they display their Long-Range Planning Boards in their classrooms, students see what is in store for them over the semester or year, understand the reason for learning basic skills and Guided Lessons, and eagerly anticipate the next Design Challenge.

3D RED TRIANGLES: A POWERFUL TOOL FOR MEMORY RETENTION

In the initial planning process, teachers prepare for their first three months of school by studying the state standards and the required curriculum for their grade level or subject area. They select three subject matter **BIG TOPICS** to develop Design Challenges with subsequent related Guided Lessons that will propel students' learning as they build a City of the Future or other contextual environment.

To visualize how a **BIG TOPIC** becomes a Design Challenge and how **small topics**, derived from a **BIG TOPIC**, become a series of interdisciplinary Guided Lessons, teachers construct three 3D Red Triangles from heavy paper stock, and invert them to become containers. They label each inverted 3D Red Triangle with a **BIG TOPIC** that they have named; they fill each 3D Red Triangle with **small topics** (written on Post-it Notes or slips of paper) that they have named as the cross-curricular Guided Lessons they must teach. Each 3D Red Triangle represents how a single 45- to 90-minute Design Challenge leads to approximately one month of student immersion in required learning.

To model the planning process, a blown-up version of a 3D Red Triangle demonstrates for teachers the relationship between a **BIG TOPIC** and the related **small topics** that fuel Guided Lessons. Given **PROTECTION** as the **BIG TOPIC** and a Design Challenge that would require students to build a Never-Before-Seen Way to Protect Citizens Living in a City of the Future, teachers form nongrade level groups to brainstorm **small topics** related to **PROTECTION** (shelters, clothing, umbrellas, skin, hair, skulls, organs, shells, nests, parents, community, government, leaders, rules and regulations). They write the **small topics** on white Post-it Notes or slips of paper. They throw their **small topics** into the oversized 3D Red Triangle, reach in, and select **a small topic** that is not their own, and discuss how they would teach that topic as a Guided Lesson at their own grade level. This can be an eye-opener, when a high school teacher, for instance, discovers how a 2nd-grade teacher's delivery of a Guided Lesson can be modified to expand the scope of the **BIG TOPIC**.

Examples of vocabulary of **BIG TOPICS**, derived from K–12 lessons as defined in the State Curriculum Framework, range from **IDENTITY** (Never-Before-Seen Creature/Avatar) and **PROTECTION** (Never-Before-Seen Shelter) to **COMMUNITY** (Never-Before-Seen Starter City) and **EQUITY** (Never-Before-Seen Government). Other **BIG TOPICS** could include **MOVEMENT, COMPETITION, DIVISION OF LABOR, SUSTAINABILITY,** and **SCARCITY**.

The Design Challenges become progressively more complex. As teachers gain proficiency in the methodology, they learn to fill and string together 5 to 10 3D Red Triangles to display a sequence of Design Challenges with Guided Lessons for each month of an entire semester or school year. They tailor their sequences to a curriculum-based "story" for students' evolving City of the Future (or a Never-Before-Seen

Community, Settlement/Colony, Ancient Civilization, Biome, Biosphere, Business, etc.).

Connecting a series of 3D Red Triangles displays a progression of monthly, **BIG TOPIC** Design Challenges that activate the growth of the interdependent parts of a student-built City of the Future.

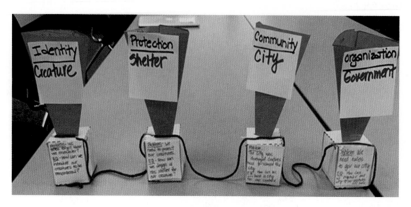

A four-month sequence of **BIG TOPIC** Design Challenges and **small topic** required Guided Lessons. The sequence order is flexible, according to teachers' subject matter requirements.

An Example of a Proposed, Four-Month, 4th-Grade Language Arts Sequence

Students write a descriptive story detailing the physical characteristics of the Never Before Seen Creature/Avatar that they built for the Design Challenge, **BIG TOPIC: IDENTITY.** The **BIG TOPIC** for the next Design Challenge is **PROTECTION.** After students build their Never-Before-Seen-Shelters to protect their Creatures/Avatars, they write about the physical characteristics of the Shelters and refer to a list of descriptive words to write about what it is like for their Creatures to live there. Students build a Never-Before-Seen Starter City for the **BIG TOPIC** Design Challenge **COMMUNITY** and write a detailed account, using their descriptive words to report about who they worked with, what materials they used, and what they built and why. For the fourth Design Challenge, **BIG TOPIC: ORGANIZA-TION**, students design and learn to implement a Never-Before-Seen Way to Govern their City and write speeches, job applications, and rules and regulations.

An example of a six-month sequence. (In this photo, teachers ran out of red card stock and improvised.)

Textbooks tell teachers to present "page 7" and have students answer the questions on "page 8," but not how to make the information on "page 7" usable and reusable in the long term. Instead of lockstep textbook instruction, starting with a **BIG TOPIC** Design Challenge opens the door to expand teaching across the curriculum. Textbooks, other source materials, and technology become resources to support students' creative and critical thinking as they are taught subject matter Guided Lessons (**small topics**) that follow each Design Challenge.

Teachers transfer the content of their 3D Red Triangles to paper or computer-generated Curriculum Integration Charts, making one Chart per Design Challenge. Each multicolored Chart documents the relationship between a **BIG TOPIC** Design Challenge and the required standards that are the basis for the content of the teacher's Guided Lessons in an integrated curriculum.

AN EXAMPLE OF 2ND-GRADE TEACHER LYNN FISHER'S CURRICULUM INTEGRATION CHART WITH STANDARDS AND GUIDED LESSONS

STANDARDS				
Language Arts	Social Studies	Math	Science	Visual and Performing Arts
Know and use various text features such as diagrams, charts, and captions. Compare the most important points presented by two texts.	Compare and contrast basic land use in urban, suburban, and rural environments.	Measure length using two different forms of unit measurements. Compare 2D shapes to 3D shapes.	Plan and conduct investigation to describe properties of different kinds of materials. Research natural disasters and their causes.	Creative Expression: Role and development of the visual arts.

BIG TOPIC: PROTECTION

Problem: The Never-Before-Seen Creatures need shelters.

Essential Question: How are people, animals, and things protected?

Design Challenge

Never-Before-Seen Shelter

Criteria List

DON'T WANTS	NEEDS	POINTS
• 2-D • Already-Been-Seen (ABS) • Too many or too few parcels • Parcel smaller than 3in x 3in and a shelter that doesn't fit • All the same shape • Magic solutions	• 3-D • Never-Before-Seen (NBS) • A way to protect the Creature from danger • The Creature must fit and be able to move inside the shelter • Every Creature has a parcel • Each parcel has a shelter • At least three different shapes • All parcels must fit within the boundaries of the map area • A way to get in and out	

GUIDED LESSONS

Small Topics

Language Arts	Social Studies	Math	Science	Visual and Performing Arts
• Create a diagram showing the Shelter's design features • Compare/contrast your Shelter to another	• Explain whether your Shelter would be best in an urban, suburban, or rural environment and why	• Measure the height/width of your Shelter using two different units of measurement • Describe Shelter in terms of which 2D shapes could be traced from the 3D Shelter	• Investigate the properties of the various materials in the Happy Trash used to build your Shelter • Create a safety plan for your Creature/ Shelter during a natural disaster	• Create a painting of your Shelter using 3D shapes • Identify and describe Shelters in famous works of art

A series of Long-Range Planning Boards display an integrated curriculum for any grade level or subject area. For each monthly Design Challenge and its related Guided Lessons, teachers fabricate a Long-Range Planning Board by refining the information from their 3D Red Triangles and their 2D Curriculum Integration Charts. The resulting 5 to 10 separate Long-Range Planning Boards encompass five months of a semester or 10 months of a school year. Basically scale-enlarged pacing guides, Long-Range Planning Boards are made of poster board or fabric with clear, 4- × 4-inch plastic pockets attached.

With a color-coded, detachable legend, Long-Range Planning Boards are portable, reusable, and easy to modify according to changing requirements. Together, they visually display a teacher's unique, cross-curricular sequence of monthly **BIG TOPIC** Design Challenges, with Essential Questions that amplify the required curriculum. The visibility of this display in the classroom enables students, parents, and

Teacher Miguel Fernandez made a clear Key for his Long-Range Planning Boards so that his 2nd graders could easily follow his monthly plans.

High school English/Art/Special Education teacher Yvette Villaseñor's Long-Range Planning Boards showing her sequence of five Design Challenges for semester-long curriculum.

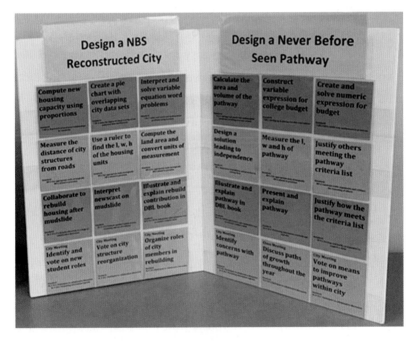

A close-up view of two Long-Range Planning Boards displaying Design Challenges with related Guided Lessons, developed by high school Math teacher Rana Masri.

administrators to see that academic requirements are being met. (See Chapter 18: Long-Range Planning Boards in Depth.)

The teachers I work with often say that their usual teaching practice is a series of fragmented topics and themes from the State Curriculum Framework, workshops, and staff development classes. They describe this fragmentation as tiring, confusing, and demeaning, and say that it doesn't ask them to be the professionals they are or give them the tools for using their own expertise. They're 100 percent right. Every time new requirements emerge from the federal government, state, and district, teachers must attend professional development trainings to learn how to plan and deliver them.

These trainings are usually not interdisciplinary. Teachers are taught how to pace sequential subject matter lessons from textbooks to engage English language learners and to teach Language Arts, Science, and Mathematics, often using these new activities and techniques for a period of time, then putting them aside when the next training occurs. Missing in these trainings is how to weave the new requirements into a sequential, integrated curriculum that will spark students' imaginations and sustain their engagement over a semester or year. Design-Based Learning teachers develop and display a sequential, in-depth course of study with the flexibility to accommodate ever-changing academic requirements.

Through all the years that my Design-Based Learning methodology has evolved, propelling me from classroom teacher to researcher and university professor, I have found one significant constant: When teachers make and display their Long-Range Planning Boards in their classrooms, they see their integrated curriculum come to life as their students anticipate each new Design Challenge, become facile at making changes and reusing learned information, experience problem seeking and problem solving as an engaging type of play, and want to participate.

I thoroughly enjoyed every second I was fortunate to be a part of the UCLA Design-Based Learning training. It was THE best training session I have attended in all my years as an educator. I left with a plethora of knowledge, but most importantly I left with an attitude that I CAN change the world. It is because of you and this methodology I am confident going into this new school year.

—Phelondra Clifford, TK–5 Art and Innovation Specialist, Learning by Design Charter School, Los Angeles Unified School District

ESSENTIALS OF THE DOREEN NELSON METHOD OF DESIGN-BASED LEARNING

The Spatial Domain/Tactile Learning

An on-ramp to creative thinking. A sequence of hands-on, nonreplicative designs built by students who become "future thinkers" as they develop a three-dimensional environment, based on a real place or system, that becomes the context for displaying their ideas and for learning the required curriculum.

Never-Before-Seen (NBS)

A nonreplicative artifact imagined and quickly built by students following preset criteria, as a solution to a real-world dilemma. The artifacts represent students' original thinking about Essential Questions found in subject matter, and are made before textbook study and comparisons to what others have historically done.

Context

A 3D City of the Future—or a Never-Before-Seen Community, Settlement/Colony, Ancient Civilization, Biome, Biosphere, Business, or any other contextual environment—rooted in reality and based on grade-level curriculum.

Backwards Thinking™

Creative thinking and self-expression start the learning process through the building of original artifacts as preparation for required Guided Lessons; artifacts are then revised through the application of learned information. By making necessary revisions, students experience how mistakes can lead to success.

Criteria List

A compilation of "Don't Wants" and "Needs." A set of requirements for a Design Challenge presented by the teacher as the "client" to the students as individual "designers" to follow as they build original artifacts. A surrogate for the teacher and a tool for assessment to hold students accountable.

Parts to Whole

Owning, fitting together, and managing individual parts of a reality-based, contextual whole (a City) presents the gestalt of the whole. Being part of designing and running a known, contextual whole for the future gives students an invested "near" experience as problem seekers and problem solvers, and takes them "far," leading to the transfer of learning of what is similar, but not the same. Students operate in many different roles simultaneously, as landowners, as citizens, as politicians, etc., to achieve a student-centered classroom where communication, collaboration, governance, and social responsibility are part of everyday learning.

Non-Specific Transfer of Learning

A process of Experimental Inquiry teaches students to use and reuse information, transferring learning from one subject area to another, and to identify powerful ideas, universal concepts, principles, values—the Essential Questions that underlie learning anything—in diverse academic and real-life settings (metacognition).

Transformations/Menu of Change™

A vocabulary for Experimental Inquiry leading to Non-Specific Transfer of Learning.

Student-Centered Classroom/Governance

Civics in action. Teaches social justice and social responsibility, and facilitates collaboration, communication, and shared decision-making. Students role-play leadership in government as Mayor, Council District Members, Commissioners, etc., for their City of the Future. In a parallel structure, students apply what they learn in those roles to comparable jobs in the classroom. They experience ways to conduct meetings, gain confidence in giving individual and group presentations, and become discerning, attentive listeners.

Long-Range Planning Boards

Sequential organization of Design Challenges and required Guided Lessons in a semester- or yearlong teaching plan. A roadmap for an integrated curriculum visible to all (students, parents, administrators, etc.); shows students a potential future and promotes accountability.

History Wall

Classroom walls become a review and a celebration of learning; a narrative of an evolving contextual story. The History Wall is to teachers what the City is to students: parts to a contextual whole.

OWNING AND REUSING

INFORMATION

Non-Specific Transfer of Learning

Look! My shoelaces are like the freeway system, because they connect the holes on my shoe, and the freeways connect places in the city!
—3rd-grade student in a Design-Based Learning class

"How do citizens want their city to look 25 years in the future?" In 1967, I was the only educator (and one of only two women) in a group of architects, planners, religious leaders, and businessmen appointed to the Los Angeles Goals Committee, an initiative started by the city's then-Mayor, Sam Yorty. We crafted and administered surveys to citizens in public places, asking for opinions about the future of Los Angeles. We collected thousands of pieces of data. The results shocked us.

When asked to imagine ways that people might move around in the future, most respondents simply described more cars, more freeways, and the possibility of a monorail. After all, Disneyland had one. Our group wanted to know why so many people surveyed were unable to envision the diverse needs of the future. I proposed trying a version of the survey with my 5th-grade students, because the lore says that kids are more creative than adults. I found the same unimaginative results. I had already started my master's degree studies and had begun in-depth research into how creative thinking could be achieved. I felt that it was a waste of time to continue working with adults when I couldn't even activate creative thinking among 10-year-olds. I thought I knew how to fix it. The work of the committee ended, but the members encouraged me to establish a systematic process that would put my findings into practice.

Wanting to teach students to think creatively, to know what they know (metacognition), and to apply **BIG TOPICS,** principles, concepts, and values named in the required curriculum, kept me constantly exploring ways to prepare them for an unknown future. I wanted them to be flexible, higher-level thinkers with the ability to own and reuse information and apply it in a variety of unforeseen contexts.

By the end of the 1960s, I was knee-deep in trying my ideas out in my classroom, and by 1971, I had formalized my Design-Based Learning methodology and was training other teachers to apply it in K–12 classrooms.

APPLE COMPUTER AND THE VIVARIUM PROJECT

In 1986, I began working with famed computer scientist Alan Kay and his Advanced Research Group from Apple Computer in the Vivarium Project at the Open Magnet Elementary School in the Los Angeles Unified School District. The Vivarium Project was not just about computers, nor was it a new curriculum or a new program. It was more an exploration for approaching the teaching and learning of complex systems and the sciences through a wide array of classroom experiences related to the existing curriculum. My work fit in, Alan felt, because "it was full of many kinds of systems thinking and other important cognitive areas, such as scaling, etc."

(I was introduced to Alan by Rachael Strickland, an architect and videographer for the Vivarium Project who had learned of my work after finding my book, *City Building Education: Transformations, Process and Theory* [1984], in the library of the Southern California Institute of Architecture, where I had taught classroom teachers.)

Alan wanted teachers to have students explore and experiment with ways of thinking both on and off the computer. I saw this as an avenue for delving further into my own research about Non-Specific Transfer of Learning. My hope was that by applying my methodology in this setting, the spatial domain would be seen as a gateway to Non-Specific Transfer of Learning and become organic to the life of the classroom so that students of any age could learn to generalize complex concepts.

Thanks to principal Bobby Blatt, the entire Open Magnet School was involved in Alan's research about teaching and learning. Apple supplied every two students with one computer embedded into a standard school desk under a glass window, with a pullout drawer for typing. Students could peer down into the computer and still use the desk for hands-on activities. (Of course, this predated laptops.) Over the next seven years, many facets of the Vivarium Project, including mine, had indirect involvement with computers, concentrating instead on understanding how to speed up the learning process. As part of this collaborative research, we applied my Design-Based Learning Methodology (then called City Building Education) in two team-taught, combined 3rd- and 4th-grade classrooms.

Alan loaded the school with "interesting people." These included Timothy Gallwey, author of *The Inner Game of Tennis*; gospel and jazz composer and multi-instrumentalist Don Lewis; composer/bassoonist John Steinmetz; the Apple Hill Chamber Players; Jill Wright, a storyteller; and Betty Edwards, who wrote *Drawing on the Right Side of the Brain*, and who could teach anyone to draw, even phobic people like me. Some of my hero educators—Neil Postman, Herb Kohl, and Jerome Bruner—joined us from time to time.

I worked with my assigned teachers, Dolores Patton and Leslie Barclay, and their combined 3rd- and 4th-grade class of 70 students once a week in a two-room bungalow called the Yellow Cluster. The first Design Challenge underscored the prominence of the building aspect of my methodology as the Yellow Cluster students, who were about to study the development of cities, built a small, rough Starter City, based on their community 100 years in the future. A limited building time of one hour ensured that their Starter City of the Future would be loaded with problems for the students to identify, research, and solve. A Criteria List named required elements of a city for evaluative purposes and stipulated that their City buildings be original and not function or look like what they saw every day. Dolores and Leslie taught the students to follow the Criteria List to assess how many requirements they had met, and once the Starter City was finished, had them name the problems they identified. (This included the fact that all of the buildings were out-of-scale).

The students' first buildings for the required population in their Starter City of the Future were mundane, replicating present-day supermarkets, shopping malls, banks, sports arenas, high-rise apartments, and freeways. Dolores asked, "Is this really what a city will look like 100 years in the future?" The students shouted, "No! This is what we have now! It's boring!" We asked, "What can you do to make your City original, and not just copy what exists now?" "How will you revise your design to serve people in the future?" "Where will the people live, and will they all live in the same kinds of places?" "Where will they work?" "Where will they shop?" "Where will they play?" "How will they move themselves and the things they need?" "Where will all of these things be in relation to one another, and why?" "What needs to be done to change the size of your buildings and be sure that all the shapes are original?"

For the rest of the school year, understanding that original answers mattered, not "right" answers, these 3rd and 4th graders had fun building inventive, Never-Before-Seen solutions to the questions we had posed and debating and getting consensus for what was to be placed in their City.

The school year was consumed with teaching students to identify and apply Non-Specific Transfer of Learning by having them experience a progressively more complex series of Design Challenges, and learn factual information based on our questions about the Starter City. Applying the critical Backwards Thinking™ process of my methodology, Dolores and Leslie used each Design Challenge as a springboard for teaching Guided Lessons in required subject matter across the curriculum (Language Arts, Mathematics, Science, Social Studies, and Civics). The students spent only a short time (60–90 minutes each week) physically building artifacts as solutions to the Design Challenges. The rest of the week was devoted to learning basic subject matter (the times tables, grammar, etc.), along with a study of curriculum-based information related to each Design Challenge. The students were taught to generalize and to use and reuse what they learned to revise their built creations and apply their thinking to other academic subjects. To ensure that Non-Specific Transfer of Learning took place, with each new Design Challenge, we kept asking them a variety of questions to teach them to analyze, synthesize, and evaluate their thinking—the higher-level thinking skills named on Bloom's *Taxonomy*.

Before wrapping up each Design Challenge, Dolores, Leslie, and I expanded the students' thinking by asking such questions as, "How would what you build affect the way people get along?" "Look, this pathway is dangerous; how can we make it safer?" "How will having this door open affect people who are walking by?" These probing questions led students to describe orally and in writing what they built, what they needed to revise, and why. Over the course of the school year, as students revised and rebuilt their designs according to new information gained from each topic they studied, the Starter City evolved into a refined City of the Future, filled with their original thinking.

"My design for 100 years in the future," said one eight-year-old student, "is a flying spinner that delivers anything in two minutes to any place in the world." (This was years before the advent of a drone delivery system!)

One student made "a weightless place to eat because it's too crowded everywhere. You get a glove with Velcro on it, and the fork has Velcro so you can hold it, and there's a plate with Velcro on the table, so it stays on, and there is a weight on the bottom of the food, so it stays on the plate."

"My special walking stairs make it so the handicapped people can come places and walk up," said another.

One 3rd-grade girl made an animal hospital that looked like a giant dog. "The extra-long tail reaches out to the home of a sick animal," she wrote, "and it brings the sick animal into the dog's stomach where it's moved slowly to the hospital so it doesn't get hurt." After she read about the human digestive process, she changed the word "stomach" in her story to "intestines."

EXPANDING THE VOCABULARY FOR INVENTION

It's simple. You just take something and do something to it. Then you do something else to it. Pretty soon, you've got something.

—**Jasper Johns, American Contemporary Artist**

I worked with Dolores and Leslie and new groups of 3rd and 4th graders in the Yellow Cluster for five years. One stumbling block we faced was the students' limited vocabulary for inventing original artifacts for their City and applying that vocabulary to basic skills in Language Arts, Math, and Science. In my research in the early 1970s, as I sought ways to promote Non-Specific Transfer of Learning, I had collected descriptive words from artists, architects, designers, mathematicians, and scientists that they associated with change. (See TRANSFORMATIONS/Menu of Change in Chapter 2.) During the years of the Vivarium Project, computer scientists and mathematicians, including Alan Kay and Seymour Papert, were among those who contributed to this descriptive vocabulary. When they approached a problem requiring a creative solution, some said that they had a kind of listing in their heads of various things to do to change what exists that might solve the problem. The list included:

1. Magnitude (size, weight)
2. Form and Space (families of form, materials, organization, light)
3. Function (purpose, behavior, movement, sound, style, portability)
4. Time
5. Place
6. Experience (point-of-view)

Usually, however, the list was not explicit. These innovators were so fluid in making change that they felt it happened automatically.

Could Yellow Cluster students access their own creative thinking by applying these specific words of change across various domains and subject areas? The Yellow Cluster teachers and I were joined by classical musician John Steinmetz, one of Alan Kay's "interesting people." John had been at the offsite learning labs attended by the Advanced Apple Research Group, consultants, and the Open Magnet School teachers, and had experienced building a City of the Future and a "New Skin" body cover to explore my methodology. He knew that I had an orchestral background as a trained harpist and together, we wanted to explore Non-Specific Transfer of Learning from the spatial domain to the aural domain.

We worked with a small, pullout group of the Yellow Cluster students for a few hours a week over several months. After students enlarged a small object of their choice to wear as a New Skin and named all of the changes involved in the construction process, they were ready for the next step in our research into Non-Specific Transfer of Learning. Since they had "composed" a new "them" by making small objects bigger to make their New Skin body covers, we asked them to do the same thing to the sounds their small objects made. John and I thought the students would struggle to do the complex thinking required to find an enlarged sound that correlated to their object. We didn't want to give them the answer by saying "Make the sound bigger." The point was to find out if the students could make the leap and transfer learned information from one setting to another.

They surprised us. A 3rd grader, whose New Skin was a book, flipped the pages of a real book with a "whoosh" sound for everyone to hear. We asked our research question: "Can you do to that sound what you did to the small book in your hand when you turned it into a New Skin?" After looking around the room for a few moments, the student and two of his peers, who were also New Skin books, leaped up, ran over to a window, and used its Venetian blinds to play an accurate, enlarged version of the sound of the small book having its pages flipped.

The following week, we had the students further explore the concept of changing from "small to big." We had them listen to and sing or say all of the sounds made by their small, original New Skin objects and put the sounds in a specific order to create their own musical compositions. We weren't teaching about music or sound. We were exploring how to teach students to internalize a specific concept learned in one area and reuse it in a new setting.

In Guided Lessons we taught them to describe different terms related to sound (loud, soft, slow, fast, intermittent, etc.). They drew pictures of all the sound variations made by their objects, and put them in an order of their choice on a 12 × 36-inch piece of paper to represent individual "musical scores." Again, we asked our research question: "Can you do to the sounds made by these small objects in your composition what you did to make a New Skin body cover?" The answer was unanimous: "We have to make all the sounds bigger." One 4th grader said, "if we want to make the sounds bigger, we all have to sing the sounds together." Everyone agreed, and they sang each other's musical scores. John taught them how to conduct the group as each student led a rehearsal of his or her own composition. As they rehearsed, the students edited their order of the sounds to improve the performance. From then on during the research project, our question "Can you do to this what you did to that?" became a serious part of the teaching and learning process. We discovered that students had no trouble moving knowledge among domains or disciplines as long as we asked them the right question. The focus of our research remained: "What are some good ways to ask?" As we observed students moving information around, we found that teaching about similarities, differences, and change led them to assimilate complex concepts easily.

We developed an exercise for students to make their own Menu of Change lists. We had them fold a piece of paper into eight squares and make a rough drawing of their New Skin object in the first square and label it "original." In each subsequent square, the students referred to their original drawing and drew and named one more change, ending up with seven different changes.

One 3rd grader, whose original New Skin object was a pencil, created a Menu of Change describing the seven changes she made to it as "chopped up," "squashed," "robot," "shrunk," "giant," "wibble-wobble," and "bounce."

No two students used the same words. We wondered if they could reuse and apply these personal words in other distinct compositional areas. In our next session, we had students use their Menu of Change words to write descriptive sentences.

The 3rd grader, whose New Skin Object was a pencil, wrote the following:

ORIGINAL	CHOPPED-UP
I liked dressing up as a pencil.	I liked dressing up as a pencil because I couldn't get chopped up by the pencil sharpener.
SQUASHED	ROBOT
I liked dressing up as a pencil but I felt squashed inside my costume.	I liked dressing up as a pencil because I felt like a robot when I walked.
SHRUNK	GIANT
I liked dressing up as a pencil because when I saw a real pencil it looked like it shrunk.	I liked dressing up as a pencil because I felt like I could make giant marks everywhere.
WIBBLE-WOBBLE	BOUNCE
I liked dressing up as a pencil when I would wibble-wobble all over the place.	I liked dressing up as a pencil with an eraser to bounce on.

We finished the session with Guided Lessons teaching students how to organize all of their sentences into original stories that summarized what it felt like to pretend to be an object.

To teach the students that they could think beyond the function of the square and rectangular buildings that they had replicated previously in their Starter City of the Future, we had them apply this Menu of Change process to the spatial domain. We focused on housing because the students had not built enough shelters for the citizens in their Starter City, and those they had built were not Never-Before-Seen. We gave each student eight pieces of shaped and tabbed white card stock that when folded formed a freestanding cube. We told them this cube was an Already-Before-Seen Shelter and had them label it "Original." We asked them to use their Menu of Change words to build seven more shelters, each with a different function. To encourage spontaneous creativity, we gradually decreased the time allotted for each Shelter: 10 minutes for the first; 2 minutes for the last.

The 3rd grader who had been the New Skin pencil had no trouble using her personal Menu of Change words as she reimagined and reshaped the original cube to build her shelters. She "chopped" her second folded cube into sections with scissors to make more living spaces. She "squashed" her third folded cube, explaining that it was a place for keeping things safe underground. She glued pieces of paper onto her fourth folded cube to make a "robot" shelter with arms as a people mover. She "shrunk" her fifth cube by folding it smaller to shelter a pet. She added another piece of card stock to her sixth folded cube to make a "giant" building "so new people coming to the City have places to live." Thinking about earthquakes, she made her seventh folded cube "wibble-wobble" on pipe cleaner rockers and rolled her last folded cube into a ball so her building would "bounce."

Over the next few weeks, the 3rd and 4th graders continued to revise their City of the Future as Dolores and Leslie guided them to observe the effects of making purposeful change. When a student was stymied about what to design for a way to move around the City or a place for recreation, for example, the teachers or fellow students would say, "Do your Menu." The students learned to pay attention to change in every corner of the curriculum. They described their reasons for applying change to the endings of stories, to wall displays, to the layouts of their classroom, and even to how they looked at mathematical equations. We often heard such comments as, "This is just like what we did the other day when we learned to change fractions!"

The Vivarium Project was an unexpected gift to my research as documented in the collaborative book on Non-Specific Transfer of Learning for Apple Computer (*Change and Creativity: A Guidebook for Teachers*, December 1992, Nelson, Doreen; Steinmetz, John; Patton, Dolores; and Barclay, Leslie). Realizing that no one was judging what I wanted to try out, I was propelled to revisit and refine the principles that operated in my methodology.

> When computers can do what Doreen has done with manual simulations, we will be somewhere. As far as I am concerned, this is the best way to get [students] ready to study the more difficult things that are the basis of the arts and sciences.
> —**Alan Kay**

THE HEART OF THE MATTER: THE WEIZMANN INSTITUTE, ISRAEL

There is a strong relationship between creative thinking and the ability to apply complex information in a variety of settings and to use that information in original ways. When I arrived at the Weizmann Institute in Rehovot, Israel in 1997, an entire multistory building devoted to K–12 Science education greeted me. I had been invited there by a group of educators to apply my Design-Based Learning, Backwards Thinking™ methodology to a study of the human heart. I walked into a room filled with expensive models depicting the relationship between the heart and the human body that were being considered for purchase to be distributed to high school classrooms throughout Israel. I said that with my methodology they wouldn't need to purchase any of them.

I grabbed a piece of paper and rolled it up and said, "This is the heart. But instead of telling students that it's the heart, present it in the context of a 'story.' Tell them it's a pump that has to move a delicate liquid to places that have both thick and thin pathways, not 'veins and capillaries.' And tell them it has to constantly clean the liquid in four different ways, rather than referring to the four chambers of the heart. With these conditions in mind, ask students to imagine how such a pumping station would function using strings of different widths attached to their rolled-up piece of paper to represent the array of pathways served by the pumping station.

"Meeting the criteria for this physical model of their own making gives students ownership of their thinking and is a tool for self-assessment. After making and justifying these rough models, students then research and compare their thinking to factual information about the human heart. The more they talk about their solutions and the more they do research, the more they refine their physical model, which becomes a mnemonic device for activating long-term memory storage so that what is learned can be used and reused—the definition of Non-Specific Transfer of Learning."

I collaborated with a team to write a Science curriculum for this study about the heart using my Design-Based Learning Backwards Thinking™ methodology. It specified how physical models built by students would lead to their understanding of such academic topics as circulation and movement systems at the macro and micro level—the movement of neurons, people, goods, the Earth, etc. This curriculum gained widespread use in Israeli high schools.

Over the more than 50 years that I have spent studying how to teach the principles, concepts, values, and Essential Questions associated with Non-Specific Transfer of Learning, the results of my research have proven definitive: teaching for Non-Specific Transfer of Learning through the spatial domain launches the higher-level thinking skills that propel creative and critical thinking. Non-Specific Transfer of Learning, embedded in my Design-Based Learning Backwards Thinking™ method, illuminates the very meaning of teaching and learning.

As my Design-Based Learning methodology evolved, propelling me from classroom teacher to researcher and university professor, I found one significant constant: when students of any age start their learning process with their own original creations based on required criteria, they become facile at making changes and reusing learned information and they come to experience problem seeking and problem solving (experimental inquiry) as an engaging type of play and want to participate.

IN A NUTSHELL

THE DOREEN NELSON METHOD OF DESIGN-BASED LEARNING IS *NOT* ABOUT . . .

. . . Design

The methodology is not for training future professional designers. It is not an art program. The word "design" is a synonym for creativity. It is a part of every subject in the academic curriculum through the artifacts that students build. Creativity for design professionals comes with constraints from the client: the criteria for what is not wanted and what is needed. In Design-Based Learning classrooms, the teacher is the "client" and the students are the "designers." The teacher's subject matter-driven Criteria List propels creativity. The Criteria List is a surrogate for teaching students to self-assess the success or failure of the artifacts they build and makes clear to them how information gained from research can improve and enhance creative ideas. Thinking creatively becomes a natural process that carries over into students' daily lives, giving them an understanding of the "why" of what they are learning.

. . . 2D

The methodology is about the spatial domain: given a **BIG TOPIC** Design Challenge, students imagine and build 3D artifacts that represent their original thinking about a specific topic. They learn to own their ideas. Adhering to the teacher's subject-based criteria, students build Never-Before-Seen (by them) imagery and teachers use that imagery to teach Guided Lessons (**small topics**) from the required curriculum. If a teacher chooses to have students do drawings, that can be a Guided Lesson that occurs after the original object is built.

. . . Specific Transfer of Learning

The methodology is not about teaching facts with limited applications (Specific Transfer of Learning). It is about teaching powerful ideas, universal concepts, principles, values, the Essential Questions that underlie learning anything, and the process of Experimental Inquiry that leads to transfer from one subject to another (Non-Specific Transfer of Learning).

. . . Small Ideas

This methodology is a pedagogy. It is not projects or a scripted curriculum. When learning starts with creativity, students are asked to think of their own Never-Before-Seen, original solutions to dilemmas before they read about how others have solved them. If the **BIG TOPIC** is **MOVEMENT**, for example, students will not be asked to build a car, truck, train, or plane as a Design Challenge. Instead, imagine the word **MOVEMENT** written on the wide top of an inverted triangle, the word **Transportation**, in the middle and the word **car** written on the pointed bottom. If students simply start at the bottom, learn about a car, and make a replication of it, they are not learning that a car was a solution to the need for a carrier to move people, goods, and services. Nor are they learning that carriers require a system of pathways in order to function. Instead, the teacher would give students a Criteria List describing the requirements for "Carriers" and present a **BIG TOPIC** Design Challenge asking for a Never-Before-Seen Way to Move People or Things or a Never-Before-Seen System for Carriers. (For a study of the circulatory system in Biology, "Carriers" would be blood cells and "Systems" would be veins and arteries.) Students formulate their original ideas guided by the teacher's Criteria List for each Design Challenge and are assessed on their ability to meet the criteria.

. . . City Studies

The methodology is about the City as a physical vehicle for learning, and the parts of the City that make up the whole are a metaphor for an integrated curriculum. It is not about teaching architecture or city planning. It is not a building "project." A roughly constructed, tabletop model of an imagined City of the Future (or a Never-Before-Seen Community, Settlement/Colony, Ancient Civilization, Biome, Biosphere, Business, etc.), based on a real location or system, becomes the setting for an ongoing "story" that brings the City to life over a semester or a school year. The "story" is a curriculum-related scenario describing the reason for building the City and what it takes to make it work: students become designers ("hired" by the teacher as their "client") to redesign their real city for a time in the distant future; they can be the first people to settle the location or they can be scientists building a biosphere. The City provides students a way in to subject matter as they build Never-Before-Seen solutions in response to a sequence of curriculum-driven, **BIG TOPIC** Design Challenges, and revise those artifacts following research and required Guided Lessons (**small topics**). They learn to continuously ask "why" questions to clarify information as they take ownership of the individual pieces they build, and interact with others while building the whole City.

The City and the tangible artifacts that are built for the City are props that spark learning. As students explore how things work or don't work in their Never-Before-Seen City, they learn that the information they acquire is transferable across a wide array of subjects and to real-life situations. Throughout the building process, students discover that their thoughts are worthwhile. They become curious about how their peers will solve the same problems they identify in their City. Once they begin reading about the **BIG TOPIC** posed by a Design Challenge, students are eager to make modifications to their Cities to meet the teacher's criteria. They don't need to be *told* to be curious or to persevere. These traits become ingrained.

> Kids don't want to let their built objects down.
> —**Francois Polifroni, 5th-grade teacher,**
> **San Gabriel Unified School District**

. . . The Traditional Frontward Information Delivery System

The methodology is not about teaching isolated subject matter. There is cross-curricular content for every artifact students build. Only *after* they build and present their artifacts are students taught the traditional Guided Lessons related to what they have built.

High school physics teacher Fatima asked her students to shake the small Starter Cities that they had built as if an earthquake were occurring, in order to determine the stability of their structures. Rigid structures broke. Others vibrated, but moved back to their original positions. Fatima described how waves carry energy from one place to another without any net movement of matter. She then had the students imagine water waves, where water moves back to its original position. Working in pairs to share ideas, her students discussed how their structures were analogous to the particles that move as energy is transferred through them. Continuing to teach backwards, Fatima found that her Design-Based Learning students were able to solve problems involving frequency, wavelength, and speed. "The students' Cities really allowed me to have something to refer to when talking about and describing wavelengths and speed," said Fatima. "It seemed like each student had something to work with, rather than just a few students who are eager to participate in my class. Students understood the analogy between their structures and the particles of a medium that waves travel through, so they were thinking at a higher level."

—2008

. . . Students Working Alone

The methodology promotes a decentralized classroom, differentiates learning, and teaches interdependence and shared problem solving. Classrooms are student-centered with the teacher as facilitator. The physical classroom shifts to accommodate the building of a small, Never-Before-Seen City, Settlement, Civilization, Biological System, etc., providing a daily visual cue for learning subject matter, and for practicing social interaction.

. . . Government

The methodology does not focus on formal government studies, nor does it promote an authoritarian classroom, where all knowledge and rules of behavior flow from the teacher and textbooks. It is about decentralizing the classroom, putting Civics in action, and promoting social responsibility. A City in the classroom is run by the students, role-playing as mayor, council members, housing commissioners, etc. Classroom management is taught as students transfer their information about City government jobs to comparable jobs in the classroom. Students are taught to make individual and group presentations, facilitating collaboration, communication, and shared decision-making.

. . . Replication

The methodology doesn't ask that students demonstrate what they know or what they need to know by replicating what others have made. Instead, after students have a go at imagining and building a Never-Before-Seen artifact that solves a real-world dilemma—before they learn how it has already been solved—they learn factual information through the teacher's Guided Lessons and compare their results with what others have historically done.

. . . Project-Based Learning

The methodology is not a curriculum or a stand-alone project. It is a pedagogy for teaching creative and critical thinking that cuts across *all* subjects to integrate the curriculum.

. . . Perfect Products

There are *no wrong answers* in the Doreen Nelson Method of Design-Based Learning. What students first build demonstrates their original thinking about what they are going to learn. Students are held accountable for their creative thinking, not for how their built artifacts look, as they describe how their artifacts solve real-world dilemmas and meet the criteria set by the teacher. After hearing the solutions of others, studying textbooks and other resource material, students continue to adhere to the required criteria as they revise their built artifacts, demonstrating their thinking about the new learning they have acquired.

THE DOREEN NELSON METHOD OF DESIGN-BASED LEARNING HAS RIGOR. IT IS *NOT* ABOUT . . .

. . . Replicating What Others Have Done

. . . Building Things and Taking Them Home

. . . Arts and Crafts

. . . Warm and Fuzzy Make-Work

. . . "What do you want to do today, dear?"

"Design-Based Learning is not traditional learning," says Los Angeles Unified School District Resource teacher Barbara Sunenshine, who teaches all subjects to grades 6 and 7. "It's 'putting the cart before the horse.' It's thinking about big topics and being creative. It's front-loading the criteria [of the curriculum] without the students knowing it. It's the 'Great Aha.' By connecting the 'Never-Before-Seen artifact' with Common Core Standards, the students develop higher-order thinking in a nonconventional way. Surprise! The students like learning, become motivated, and become more inventive."

Goodbye to Formulaic Teaching

After writing eloquently about what she had observed while visiting Design-Based Learning classrooms as an undergraduate, a teacher just starting her career dropped out of the two-year Design-Based Learning master's degree program, saying, "Design-Based Learning is for every kid, but not for every teacher."

When I asked the other teachers in her group what they thought she meant, opinions varied:

"Some long-time teachers settle into a classroom practice and aren't comfortable with change."

"Some feel that it will be too difficult for students to understand."

"Some teachers assume it is about art-making or project-based learning and they already do that."

"Or," said one of the most seasoned teachers in the group, "they are skeptical, as I was before coming into the Design-Based Learning MA program. Because by the time I learn what new teaching practice is in the current vogue, something else replaces it. And if you don't like teaching a program that one administrator pushes you to teach, you wait it out until either that principal leaves or the program itself goes out of style. It's no wonder students suffer and learning doesn't stick.

"But Design-Based Learning," he observed, "is a methodology, not 'projects.' That is making all the difference for me and for my students—and learning a flexible teaching methodology makes me feel like a creative professional."

Teachers returning to learning-by-doing say that they are attracted to my methodology because they feel that something is missing from their teaching practice. They are tired of hearing their students ask, "What will I ever use this for?" They are aching for solutions to the boredom they feel and want to find ways to engage themselves and their equally bored students to ensure learning success in *all* subjects. The same is true for teachers trying to engage nonverbal students and others with severe learning disabilities.

Universities, book companies, and people in power, who give money and start schools, claim to know how to "fix" education. Their solutions for professional teacher trainings and staff developments lean heavily toward spoon-fed, pre-digested experiences.

It troubles me that teaching is not thought of as an art and that teachers are not thought of as educator-artists. I want teachers to feel comfortable, energized, and focused as they learn something new, and to know that they can make mistakes as they learn. Mistakes and revisions are part of the creative process and everyday life.

In the early to mid-twentieth century, education was a hot topic in the United States, due to John Dewey, a towering figure in American education. In 1897, with the transformative effect of the Industrial Age on jobs and careers in full sway, Dewey famously said, "Education is a process of living, not preparation for future living." For him, school needed to mirror an evolving society. For decades, Dewey's principles of education reigned across the nation.

Dewey's "learning by doing" philosophy was embraced by teacher training institutions and was a guiding force in public education until 1957. His philosophy fueled the creation of such landmark institutions as the experimental and interdisciplinary Black Mountain College in North Carolina (1933–1957), which drew iconoclastic artists Arnold Schoenberg, John Cage, Merce Cunningham, Joseph and Anni Albers, Robert Motherwell, Jasper Johns, and Walter Gropius among many others.

Then what happened? In 1957, Sputnik went up. The history-making launch of the Russian spacecraft sparked America's determination to compete with the then-U.S.S.R. and suddenly science and math took a dominant role in teacher education. Teaching students the scientific method was vital, assessing student learning consumed the nation's schools, and the social sciences and the arts became an afterthought.

This section describes ways that teachers have applied my Design-Based Learning, Backwards Thinking™ methodology to break out of formulaic teaching. As they left their comfort zone to express their own creative thinking in the delivery of the curriculum, their classrooms became places where learning jumped off the page.

"I'M NOT CREATIVE"

Each year, the kindergarten students in Beverly Piper's class couldn't wait to dress up in costumes they designed to celebrate Chinese New Year. That was the best way to teach about cultural celebrations, Beverly said, adding that her students liked making their costumes and pretending that they lived in China. She wasn't happy when I persisted in asking, "What was the question that these costumes answered? Did your students learn the concept of cultural celebrations, or simply replicate costumes worn to celebrate Chinese New Year?"

Beverly was in the first Design-Based Learning master's program cohort group at Cal Poly Pomona in 1995. To begin using her innate creative abilities, she just needed the spark of motivation provided by group discussions. To expand her young students' understanding of multicultural traditions—and to focus on pedagogy and methodology rather than a project—Beverly came up with a memorably creative approach to teach them that different people celebrate beginnings in different ways.

Instead of limiting her teaching about multiculturalism to Chinese New Year, Beverly applied my methodology and met the curriculum requirements by having her students bring a favorite toy to class and design a Never-Before-Seen Holiday for the toy to celebrate. She asked them what they thought would make their toys want to celebrate a new year, then had the students dress up in full-length ponchos made from old sheets that she had collected and cut up. Using markers, they covered the ponchos with pictures representing the New Year hopes of their toys.

The result: the "turtle" celebrated a clean place to live by drawing a broom and a cloth on his poncho and wearing white gloves. The "Barbie Doll" celebrated a year without broken parts by drawing all of the parts on the poncho and carrying a photo of her intact doll. The "teddy bear" celebrated getting washed by making a drawing of his teddy bear tucked into a washing machine. Finally, after all the students' costumes were ready to be paraded around the school campus, Beverly showed the class photos of people celebrating Chinese New Year. The kindergartners made the connection immediately, saying, "That's just like us, Mrs. Piper!" Afterward, in Guided Lessons, Beverly taught her students about different celebrations throughout the world, and had them bring examples of New Year celebrations from their own cultures to share with the class.

Beverly, who succumbed to an illness before graduating from the program, left a legacy of unique Design Challenges for other teachers.

When teachers studying Design-Based Learning announce right off the bat that they are not creative, I wince. Clearly, they are! Their need to ensure that the required curriculum sticks with their students drives them to want to do things differently. The open-ended possibilities of my 6½ Steps of Backwards Thinking™—a process of design, research, and revision—inspire teachers to call on their own creative powers to select and deliver information through a sequence of Design Challenges and related subject-matter Guided Lessons that amplify their required curriculum. The question that some ask during this process—"Can't you just tell me if you liked or didn't like what I did, or if I did it right?"—disappears as teachers recognize and claim their own creativity.

Rana Masri, a Math teacher at Delmar High School, Model Continuation School in the San Gabriel Unified School District, said the methodology was a lifesaver during the Covid-19 pandemic, which made virtual learning a necessity. (See "In the Virtual Classroom" in Chapter 3.) "Creative thinking is something that has become consistent in my online classroom. Not only does Design-Based Learning ask my kids to think creatively on a regular basis, I'm able to teach them to problem-solve so they can see how a subject that may seem abstract and foreign becomes relevant to something they are actually building, and makes factual information their own. Constant collaboration and interaction online pushes them out of their seats to become builders and storytellers in a Math class . . . and I learned how to be creative myself."

Teachers are natural designers, whether they know it or not. Designers solve problems and organize their designs to satisfy a need. Teachers do, too. They solve the design problem of how to organize the physical and virtual classroom. They design and connect lessons, and they confront a teacher's biggest design dilemma: how to make learning subject matter fun and make it stick, while satisfying school administrators and parents, despite being inundated with "new" and changing academic requirements.

Mandatory teacher trainings can be confusing, contrary, and misleading. Think about food: we know how and what to eat. Or do we? Cow's milk or soy milk? Eat fish, it's healthy. Don't eat fish, it's loaded with mercury. Cut down on carbs, load up on carbs. Don't drink coffee, it's harmful. Do drink coffee, it protects against disease. What teachers are told can be just as contradictory: follow a prescribed, lockstep subject matter curriculum and yet at the same time, present students with open-ended dilemmas so they can learn to think creatively and critically and persevere in seeking and solving problems.

The mandated Common Core Standards Initiative, launched in 2009, left teachers casting about for ways to teach student-centered lessons and meet the required four "Cs": Communication, Collaboration, Creativity, and Critical Thinking (21st Century Skills) and make them compelling: a game for spelling, a coloring book for Math facts, a video about a foreign country.

Summoned by their school district to take one training after another, teachers go home overwhelmed, frustrated, and confused by many presenters who themselves are looking for ways to hold teachers' interest. Teachers receive little follow-up coaching as they try to implement what they learn. There is limited time carved out for the regular exchange of ideas with peers, to describe their approaches to teaching the material, get feedback, and explore the intellectual underpinnings in the field of education.

"I've been teaching for 15 years," said one teacher, "and nobody has ever asked me to think about what my field is all about and the difference between pedagogy, methodology, and a project."

In their search for ways to make learning relevant, teachers can become curriculum junkies. It takes time for teachers to develop their own plans ("We're studying Japan and there's someone from Japan living next door to me. I'll ask her to come to the classroom and talk about her life in her home country"). It takes time for teachers to design ongoing student-centered experiences that stick in students' brains, but teachers love finding creative ways to impart "forever" information and to see growth in students' thinking.

The Design-Based Learning, Backwards Thinking™ methodology gives teachers the freedom to express their creativity in how they teach subject matter. They like that their plans are not cast in concrete and that they can easily alter their sequence of Design Challenges as new requirements or grade levels come along. Design-Based Learning gives them a versatile, contextual playing field—situated in an evolving "story"—for teaching across the curriculum, facilitating classroom management, making information reusable, and elevating student test scores.

CHAPTER

8

A RETURN TO THE SANDBOX

Play is the highest form of research.

—Albert Einstein

Before the start of a Design-Based Learning Summer Institute for K–12 Teachers at ArtCenter College of Design in Pasadena, California, I was in the bathroom, locked in one of the stalls, when I heard one participant telling another teacher how she felt about staff development trainings: "I hate this kind of thing," she said. "They make you do all kinds of stuff as if you're a little kid, then tell you to go back to your class and do the same thing."

There I was, the leader of the training, trapped and listening to how much this teacher didn't want to participate in what her school had paid for and required all faculty to attend.

She never knew that I had heard her. Over the next three days, I was not surprised to see her go from disliking play to being one of the best "players" in her group. She enjoyed the fact that she wasn't spoon-fed "right" answers. She became mayor of the small Starter City that her group built, and when the teachers wrote stories explaining what they made and why, her story was the most imaginative. She and her group even planned and carried out an event to commemorate their efforts with original dances and artworks. They made brochures to advertise their Starter City, and just as students in Design-Based Learning classrooms sometimes do, they prepared speeches as if they were tour guides for visitors to their City.

In the debriefing sessions, this "reluctant" participant passionately discussed the value of "play" for teaching higher-level thinking across the required curriculum, and she identified dozens of Guided Lessons related to each Design Challenge that she had experienced.

Over my decades of training teachers, and training trainers, I've developed a great deal of empathy for the resistance to play. I get it, because I once felt that way, too. In a Design-Based Learning classroom, play, which can seem arbitrary, even risky, has intellectual rigor and is deliberate. Teachers who stick with it, with or without the full support of their administrators, say that they are determined to do so because of the results they see with their K–12 students. These results inspire them to use the Design-Based Learning methodology for teaching English, History, Geography, Math, and Science—and for English-language learners and students with learning disabilities—in unique and ever-more creative ways.

Academic play through Design Challenges is a cross-curricular "sandbox" for developing the higher-level thinking skills associated with creativity.

BREAKING OUT OF THE COMFORT ZONE

When I had to present my solution to the first Design Challenge, I was really nervous that I had done it wrong. Once I started talking with my group and saw that everyone's solution was valid, I realized that I can do this! It forced me out of my comfort zone.

—Middle School Teacher, Design-Based Learning Summer Institute for K–12 Teachers, ArtCenter College of Design, 2014

Brian, a middle school music teacher who both wrote and performed popular music, came into the Design-Based Learning MA program certain that he could adapt the methodology to teaching music appreciation. He was so enthusiastic that I had him meet with John Steinmetz, the classical music composer and bassoonist I had worked with in the Apple Computer Vivarium Project. (See Chapter 5.) John had successfully applied my methodology in classes for professional musicians and music administrators.

Brian started off with a bang by developing his own sequence of Design Challenges. He began by having his students find and record a sound in their community that had a personal meaning for them.

Following some of what John and I had done in our work for Apple Computer, Brian had his students use those sounds to create and perform a Never-Before-Seen Musical Piece that he called, "The Neighborhood." He even planned a sequence of Design Challenges that would culminate in a short, collaborative, Never-Before-Seen Opera, but he ultimately felt this would be too ambitious for his daily 45-minute music appreciation class. (In retrospect, the word "Opera" may have added to his hesitation.) Brian had studied the pedagogy underlying my methodology and wanted it for his students, but he was apprehensive about fielding students' Design Challenge solutions and mistakes leading up to the opera and he returned to his familiar teaching practice.

Fifth-grade teacher Filman called me one day to say that he had come into the Design-Based Learning master's program after dropping out of an MA program in the field of school administration. He told me that he had realized being an administrator would take him away from what he loved most: his students. Fil confided that he felt a kind of calling to "save the world" by teaching his students to think using my methodology, so they could realize their full potential and thrive. Many teachers studying my methodology say something similar. What keeps me going is that each teacher applying my methodology represents my own desire to "save the world." Every year, hundreds of students benefit from these teachers who are inspiring them to be learners and creative, critical thinkers.

When I asked Fil if he was applying my methodology in his classroom, he apologized, saying that he had been too busy with other requirements. I asked if it was really because he felt nervous about implementing the process and Fil candidly agreed. He was unsure his "very difficult" students had the ability to work together and to learn from his planned mistakes, and he was afraid they wouldn't like it.

"The idea of sharing control of the learning process with students can stymie teachers," said kindergarten teacher Natalie Bezdjian, who graduated in the Cal Poly master's program in 2012 and trained all of the teachers in her private Armenian school in Design-Based Learning. She became a faculty member at ArtCenter College of Design for the Design-Based Learning Summer Institute for K–12 Teachers, and team-taught with colleagues in the Design-Based Learning MA program. "To have students come up with problems, to have them collaborate to find solutions to those problems," she said, "and to find ways to guide them through the process, requires letting go and using what happens in each Design Challenge to teach what you need to teach.

"My biggest hurdle in teaching other teachers," Natalie said, "has been to provide them with the support and confidence that they need to apply the Design-Based Learning methodology with the understanding that it will all come together, even when it feels like it takes time away from teaching, or that it feels uncomfortable."

CHAPTER

10

IT TAKES COURAGE

Although it was scary at first, I stepped outside the "traditional way of learning" box, because I wanted a way to reach all students without their thinking they will fail. You can't fail with Design-Based Learning.
—Elementary school teacher, Design-Based Learning Summer Institute for K–12 Teachers, 2011

Everyone *says* that thinking outside the box is valuable, but it takes courage to actually go outside the box and do something different.

Emily Tilton, a Language Arts and History teacher in an underserved Title I middle school in the Inland Empire, was in the sixth cohort group in the 1999 MA program with other K–12 teachers at Cal Poly, Pomona. Once a week, the class began with teachers describing how they had applied the Design-Based Learning methodology in their classrooms and what the results had been.

Emily came to one class upset. "My principal sent me a letter saying that my classroom looked like it belonged in kindergarten and demanded that I put a stop to it," she said. Emily had invested so much time and money in the master's program, I reluctantly suggested that she complete her degree by doing a traditional research project rather than applying Design-Based Learning in her classroom.

"But my students love learning this way, and I love teaching them this way," Emily tearfully told her colleagues. "They're doing better than ever before. I'm having fewer behavior problems, so I have more time for teaching. They're willing to do drill and practice after they build and govern their City, the textbooks make sense to them, and they're passing tests."

In those days, I was uneasy about working with middle school and high school teachers, even though I had taught my Design-Based Learning methodology at those grade levels years earlier. Secondary teachers are riveted on subject matter and I worried that perhaps asking them to have their students "play" as a way to achieve mastery of subject matter could be a far reach. Emily's distress over her principal's letter made it clear that wasn't the case.

She insisted that I see for myself, and when I came to her History class, what I saw was dynamic. Students were collaborating on building things for their City, they were reading books and comparing what they built to what others had done, and justifying their designs in discussions and writing. Emily had her students eating out of her hand. I couldn't comprehend why the administration didn't recognize her results. I suggested that since I was a university professor, it might make a bigger impact if we both met with her principal to explain the pedagogy and methodology of Design-Based Learning.

We developed a game plan that included my spending time in Emily's classroom to document what she was doing, and working with her to make a chart that we called the Curriculum Integration Chart (see Chapter 4), to show how she used the building of a tabletop City to deliver the required state standards in her History and Language Arts classes. We wrote a separate Curriculum Integration Chart for each subject she taught. (The clarity of the Curriculum Integration Chart continues to serve all of the teachers who are learning to apply my Design-Based Learning methodology.)

The meeting with the principal felt like an inquisition. Four high-level representatives from the School District office, along with the principal and vice-principal, faced us with a barrage of questions. Emily took control, presenting her Curriculum Integration Charts, which meticulously named the number from the State Standards Framework for each academic requirement that her students had successfully achieved.

Most of the questions had to do with the usual worries of the administration: "Are the students learning?" and "How do you know?" Others were completely off the mark: the curriculum specialist complained that when she visited Emily's classroom she saw no evidence of her teaching Language Arts and that it seemed as if the class were a free-for-all.

"Oh," Emily responded (more politely than I would have), "that was because you visited my History class and not my Language Arts class. My students were learning the History and Social Science State Standard 6.1:3—discussing human modifications of the physical environment."

Emily made it clear that she would not go back to what had been an ineffectual method of teaching. (She also addressed the accusatory tone of the principal's letter as perhaps needing mediation from the Teacher's Union.)

In the end, it was agreed that Emily could continue using Design-Based Learning in her classroom . . . with a warning that she would be watched, even though her students were excelling.

Emily went on to become a lecturer in the master's degree program at Cal Poly, and in 2002 was part of a team that launched the five-day, intensive Design-Based Learning Summer Institute for K–12 Teachers at ArtCenter College of Design in Pasadena. Over time, she refined her Design-Based Learning practice, yet despite her students' regular, high test results, she was continually asked to justify everything that she did, and although she was a tenured teacher, Emily ultimately decided to leave that district. She concluded that what she believed in was what mattered, even if it meant giving up tenure.

Not long after her decision, I got a call from the principal at a school in the district where Emily had applied to teach. I told him that Emily was a marvelous teacher, and that if he hired her he was getting a thoroughbred, who shouldn't be expected to be like the other horses in the stable. (I had just finished reading the book *Seabiscuit*, which may explain my comparison!) Appreciate Emily for what she is, I told the principal, and she will outperform everyone. He would have a showcase classroom and she would train other teachers to do the same.

When I visited her at her new school, Emily was a star, leading others to become stars, too. Now living in Oregon, Emily teaches at a Waldorf School where she has the same students from 6th to 9th grade. With her administrator's support, Emily has easily coupled the Waldorf methodology with my Design-Based Learning methodology, having her students build a different City each year, characterized by an evolving new story tied to grade-level curriculum.

CHAPTER

11

WHEN ADMINISTRATORS GET IT

The Design-Based Learning methodology is the context for all the programs in our district.

—Dr. Tiffany Rudek, Deputy Superintendent, Educational Services, San Gabriel Unified School District, 2018

Jennifer Sorbara developed and leads the Academic Design Program for 10th–12th graders at Walnut High School in the Walnut Valley Unified School District using my Design-Based Learning methodology. The program integrates Math, Social Science, History, and Language Arts. In 2017, during the Western Association of Schools and Colleges (WASC) accreditation renewal, observers came to Walnut High to evaluate schoolwide practices and plans. "One observer came to my class in the morning," Jennifer said, "and two more in the afternoon. The gist of their questions was 'Why isn't everyone else being innovative with instruction?'"

Since 1997, Jennifer's district administrators, led by different superintendents and a changing governing board, have maintained their support for widespread use of the Doreen Nelson Method of Design-Based Learning. They oversaw the construction of a building dedicated solely to the Design-Based Learning program at Chaparral

Middle School, made it possible for Jennifer to develop the program at Walnut High, and paid for teachers to attend the Summer Institute for K–12 Teachers at ArtCenter College of Design for training in the methodology. Like Jennifer, a number of Walnut Valley teachers completed the master's degree program at Cal Poly.

Other administrators "get it," too.

When teachers in the master's program learned to make detailed Long-Range Planning Boards (see Chapters 4 and 20), they were required to present and describe them to their school administrators for feedback. Often, administrators would say, "This is exactly what I want every teacher to do." Some told teachers that presenting their usual weekly lesson plans was no longer necessary, because, as one administrator said, "You clearly know where you're going and how to achieve the requirements."

Middle school Science teacher Lindsay Downs at Santa Fe High School in the Whittier Union High School District is devoted to having her special needs students achieve a mainstream education. She received her tenure in her district after graduating from the Design-Based Learning master's program in 2013. Her previous training to become a credentialed teacher hadn't provided her with the time to explore the intellectual aspects that underlie teaching and learning. She said that the MA program gave her what she had been missing.

Lindsay's principal saw that her special needs students were able to make connections between Science and other content areas through her use of Design-Based Learning's City-building theme. He witnessed first-hand the growth in her students' critical thinking and social skills as they built their City and role-played its governance and learned to process information by sharing their thoughts and ideas.

Just as significantly, this supportive principal observed Lindsay's progress as a teacher. "He told me that he wished more teachers would take the risks that I have," Lindsay said. "It was nice to have someone on the 'outside' see my personal growth and validate that what I am doing with my students is actually working."

Lindsay's administrator got it. In my experience, knowledgeable, insightful, and supportive administrators like this are not rare.

The San Gabriel Unified School District, comprising eight K–12 schools, definitely gets it. In the District, with its focus on twenty-first-century learning, my method of Design-Based Learning is the expectation and is built into the District's Strategic Plan. Since 2018, the District has offered teachers unparalleled administrative support in encouraging them to take risks and embrace change in order to create better classrooms through the methodology. In the first year of implementing Design-Based Learning district-wide, SGUSD sent administrators as well as teachers to the Design-Based Learning Five-Day, Summer Institute for K–12 Teachers at ArtCenter College of Design. By the summer of 2019, approximately 50 teachers in the District had trained in Design-Based Learning; that year, the District became the first to sign on when UCLA's Center X, one of the nation's most prestigious teacher training institutions, added Design-Based Learning to its teacher training programs. The SGUSD contract with Center X encompassed a training of trainers program for the 2020–2021 school years, and the formation of a group of "DBL Ambassadors" whose members conduct regular Design-Based Learning trainings for all the K–12 teachers in the District.

CHAPTER

12

TRY A LITTLE TRICKERY

(IT WORKS)

There we were, a group of classroom teachers, computer scientists, and musicians, standing on a hot tennis court in New Hampshire. Renowned tennis pro Tim Gallwey, author of the book, *The Inner Game of Tennis*, was facing a woman across the net who had never played before. It was 1990, and we were guests of Apple Computer's senior fellow Alan Kay, as we had been for summers since 1986, to spend one week at an off-site educational lab exploring the relationship between technology and the process of teaching and learning. In Kay's definition of technology, a tennis racquet, like a pencil, a musical instrument—or a student-built City in the classroom—is a tool of possibility.

Tim Gallwey had met us at the tennis court to demonstrate his thinking. He began by telling the woman to not think about playing tennis and didn't even give her a tennis racquet. Instead, he asked her to tell him where she thought the balls that he was sending over the net would land. She did, never missing a location. Tim then invited her to use a racquet to hit a ball back to him. She took a swing and her arm was so cramped that we all wanted to yell, "For god's sake, open your arm!" Tim said nothing about her arm. He asked the woman how her toes felt. "All cramped up," she answered. "Concentrate on relaxing your toes this time," Tim instructed her.

Voilà! The perfect swing . . . and the woman said her toes felt much better.

It was clear what Tim was doing on a very deep level. Anyone trying to persuade a reluctant baby to eat soon learns the trick of pretending the spoon is an airplane coming in for a landing or makes funny faces so that a child's mouth opens in laughter. Tim didn't want to shake the woman's confidence by critiquing her arm position. He "tricked" her into being successful so that she came away from the experience feeling that playing tennis could be fun and its mechanics were in her grasp.

The Design-Based Learning methodology calls on the same kind of "trickery," leading students to learn to be creative thinkers who retain what they learn and can apply it in other settings.

"When I first got into teaching, I envisioned creating a classroom full of wonder and creativity," said Gabriel Cabrera, a 5th-grade teacher at Washington Elementary in the San Gabriel Unified School District. "My first year of teaching was in 2006, five years into No Child Left Behind and year two of program improvement for my school, and test scores were the priority, specifically for English Language Learners. For months, I focused my efforts on doing after-school English Language Development and test preparation. I organized my teaching around the state testing. The test scores went up a bit, but my interest in teaching was fading. Earning a Master of Arts degree in Education only fed my suspicion that we were doing things wrong."

After four years, hoping to find more meaning in his profession, Gabriel "jumped" at an opportunity to teach History at a Continuation High School. He earned a single subject credential; a year later, his position was eliminated. Gabriel was assigned to teach a combined 4th- and 5th-grade GATE (Gifted and Talented Education) class of high achievers.

"I did a GATE certification program, led a Science Olympiad team's Robotics competition, did a GLAD professional development training in language acquisition and literacy, a UCLA Writing Project, and a training in the Daily 5 literacy framework—and along the way, I lost steam and interest because it didn't spark what I set out to do in teaching."

Gabriel began thinking of changing his profession. He explored other occupations and even received a job offer in the film industry, he said. "But, I decided that I needed to give teaching another chance to prove itself." In 2018, Gabriel attended the five-day, intensive Design-Based Learning Summer Institute for K–12 Teachers at ArtCenter College of Design in Pasadena.

"I thought that this could be something fun to add to my tool belt," he said. "I had been disregarding some of the textbook lessons and using my prior training to piece together a nice 5th-grade experience for my students. I had also done what I thought of as 'design' projects. I was in for a shock when I discovered that Design-Based Learning would not be just another addition to my tool belt, but an all-in-one power tool. It could be a complete overhaul of my teaching if I did the work and jumped all the way in," he said. "Doreen often refers to her Design-Based Learning 'Backwards Thinking' methodology as sneaking up on learning, a 'trick,' but I see it as a gift to students who have been longing for school to be something other than what it has been for them."

* * *

"Let me tell you about the worst group of students in the history of my elementary school," said Leakana Nhem, a 3rd-grade teacher at Willard International Baccalaureate and Technology Magnet Elementary School in the Pasadena Unified School District.

"Every teacher from kindergarten, 1st grade, and 2nd grade would say, 'Wait until you get them!' I would hear about their bad behavior every day at lunch. They misbehaved, didn't listen, talked out of turn, and couldn't sit still.

"The 2nd-grade teachers would send some of these unruly children to my room to 'cool off' every once in a while and I would ask each one what had merited the punishment. One had thrown his shoes up onto the roof of the school and arrived in my classroom shoeless. He said, 'I don't know why I did it.' One student had pinched her neighbor because his talking bothered her; she didn't know any other way to communicate her frustration. Another had bolted out of his teacher's classroom after throwing an attention-seeking fit.

"Their teachers had given up on these students," Leakana said. "When 105 of them reached the 3rd-grade level, I was given 27 of the 'worst' of them."

Rather than teaching these difficult students as they had been taught for the past three years, Leakana was determined to "trick" them into learning.

"I planned lots of Design Challenges that made my students feel as if they were playing," she said. "I had them create 3D solutions to problems in a simulated, future community as they built a small City we called 'Microdena,' because it was a smaller version of our city, Pasadena."

Why a community?

"Because they could spend the entire year forming committees," Leakana said, "evaluating problems, building solutions, and analyzing their results, while at the same time, using skills required of them from every subject area in the 3rd grade."

Why a community of the future?

"Because it forced them to think creatively to come up with Never-Before-Seen solutions. My students learned that there were many possible outcomes to a problem and that they couldn't be wrong—as long as they could justify their designs according to my Criteria List that guided them to think creatively within my constraints."

Leakana emphasized that she remained in charge of the curriculum and the students' learning. "They just didn't know it. I snuck up on them with fun and tricked them into behaviors that I wanted by asking for their opinions about everything, from what they made to running the classroom and the City.

"This group of 'horrible' students learned to work together better than any other class I had ever had in my 15 years of teaching. They learned to help each other, because they connected their lives in the classroom to the simulated community in the City that they built. They became confident and independent, identifying problems and advocating for their proposed solutions by meeting, voting, compromising, and discussing issues democratically. Because I forced them to seek and solve problems, they learned how to cope when a problem arose. Their new-found commitment and good behavior did not change even when I was absent for seven days."

What will these "worst" students remember in a few years?

"Much more than their multiplication tables and how to write a paragraph," Leakana said. "They will remember the story of a make-believe City that held their imaginations for an entire year. So much so, that they willingly composed narratives and expository texts about it, performed calculations related to its carrying capacity, conducted experiments regarding its adherence to safety and building codes, and created artwork to commemorate its existence.

"Building and rebuilding solutions all year long drove them crazy and they loved it. The test scores for these students were the highest in my school," Leakana said. "Before I applied Design-Based Learning, 85 to 89 percent of my students were proficient or advanced in Math. It's now 100 percent."

Other teachers at her school, seeing Leakana's test scores rise every year as she used the methodology, expressed interest in Design-Based Learning, but were concerned about the time and effort it would take to learn to apply it in their classrooms and felt they didn't have enough space for the students to build a City.

Leakana had learned to teach other teachers by studying with me, as Emily had. She taught Design-Based Learning in the MA program at Cal Poly and at the five-day, intensive Design-Based Learning Summer Institute for K–12 Teachers at ArtCenter College of Design. She knew she could give teachers at her school a different perspective.

"I advertised. I led trainings and workshops for my school that were related to creating an integrated curriculum. I invited teachers to my classroom where my students acted as tour guides for our History Wall and the Microdena City. The district superintendent dropped in on my classroom, and at his next board meeting described what he saw, saying that every class should be taught this way. Members of the International Baccalaureate Organization visited and wanted to learn how to do what I was doing. I kept hearing that people liked what was going on in my classroom and they wanted to know how they could do this, too."

Leakana led staff development for teachers in her school and district, establishing a pipeline of Design-Based Learning teachers. In the 2013–2014 school year, Leakana and high school Science teacher Richard Rosa from her district joined me in a five-session training for all of the district's K–12 administrators. Leakana and Richard insisted that the administrators "play" just like the kids. (Both became graduates of Cal Poly's doctoral program in Educational Leadership.)

Imagine leading a training for all of the administrators you work for. Richard and Leakana didn't flinch. They had the administrators select an object and pretend to be that object, and then had them share their stories with the others in the group. Leakana brought her 3rd graders and Richard brought his high school Science students to present their own stories about the same Design Challenge. The administrators were stunned by the degree of detail and the level of confidence that all of the students exhibited in describing their own creations.

This became the first in a series of trainings in the district, and led to a large number of teachers using all or parts of the Design-Based Learning methodology. The support of their administrators mattered; one administrator had every class in her school build a City.

"BUT I ALREADY DO THIS"

While being taught the fundamentals of the Design-Based Learning methodology in the five-day Summer Institute for K–12 teachers at ArtCenter, high school Math instructor Bharat Parekh said "But, I already do this," referring to his practice of sustaining student engagement through projects; still, he enrolled in the master's program at Cal Poly to deepen his understanding of the Design-Based Learning methodology and its use of academic "play."

Bharat candidly admitted that he had come to Design-Based Learning assuming that he knew what the methodology was all about. It was thanks to the support and patience of his cohort group and instructors, he said, that he stayed with the program, learned the difference between isolated projects and a cohesive sequence of Design Challenges, and got his master's degree.

"When I first attempted Design-Based Learning in my classroom," Bharat said, "I had trouble setting the criteria for a Design Challenge and defining my Essential Questions. I would accomplish one step, then fail with the next, trying to merge the methodology's 6½ Steps of Backwards Thinking™ into the Math curriculum, instead of figuring out how to use the methodology to *deliver* Math."

Working past his frustration, Bharat developed 10 interlinked and sequential Design Challenges. He engaged his students in the Math curriculum by having them build and develop a three-dimensional, Never-Before-Seen, tabletop City that he called "Gaxarian."

Bharat applied the methodology in two of his 10th-grade Math classes during the school year. Through his **BIG TOPIC** Design Challenges students learned to apply deductive and inductive reasoning, a core strategy in foundational geometry. The results far exceeded Bharat's expectations.

"After an anxious period of trial-and-error," he said, "I managed to restructure my classroom setting, implement a student-centered classroom, and restrategize my teaching style to change the way I delivered information. It wasn't easy. I had a lot to learn—and unlearn. I tried out many ideas I heard from my cohort group in the MA program."

Bharat created a cluster-type seating plan in his classroom to encourage cooperative learning as the students teamed up to design their three-dimensional artifacts for their City. At first, to his dismay, the new seating arrangement increased the noise level in the classroom.

"It wasn't a smooth transition for any of us, and in the initial stages of these big changes, there were times that my confidence was shaken," Bharat said. "My Design-Based Learning master's cohort and instructors encouraged me to be patient and continue experimenting."

Bharat delegated responsibilities to teams of students for classroom management and for the governance of their City of Gaxarian.

"To teach my students to take responsibilities for their decision-making, I had them set classroom protocols by asking such basic questions as 'how do you want me to treat you and why,' 'how do you think I want to be treated and why' and 'what are the basic rules and consequences that we need to establish in the classroom to maintain structure, and why?'

"How the students would communicate with one another, and how they would organize the classroom, were questions decided and voted on. They used these protocols to carry out Gaxarian 'town meetings' as well. I was even able to incorporate mathematical thinking by having students apply deductive and inductive reasoning to their meetings."

Bharat said that teaching Math became a collaborative effort and his students excelled. What seemed to take time away from his Math instruction—teaching about the governance of the classroom and the City—did just the opposite.

"For every Design Challenge, I had my students work in groups to teach them to collaborate. They learned to follow the Criteria Lists that I developed to familiarize them with the vocabulary of specific mathematical theories. I also relied on Bloom's *Taxonomy* to teach higher-level thinking skills by asking key questions about what they built as solutions to my Design Challenges. During my Guided Lessons, I taught my students to apply mathematical theories to all aspects of their Gaxarian community.

"With the completion of the fourth Design Challenge," Bharat said, "the students' points of view and their input had become the catalyst for a smoothly functioning classroom. Even students who rarely participated in the past engaged in making decisions and debating with their peers about the logic and validity of various mathematical solutions."

The high achievers in Bharat's class became mentors and took leadership roles to ensure that everyone in their groups succeeded in the Math-related performance tasks, "and I no longer felt the need to act as an authoritarian teacher," Bharat said. "I had become a facilitator. Yes, I had to adjust to the fact that this approach required that my questioning skills had to be very strategic to obtain the desired results. But the more 'why' questions that I asked related to a Design Challenge, and the more creative my students' responses were, the more motivated I was to continue promoting higher levels of thinking.

"I learned what I had resisted at the beginning of the Design-Based Learning master's program: to accept the fact that there are many ways to get to a right answer."

By applying Design-Based Learning in his classroom, Bharat was in alignment with 21st Century Skills and came to view students as creative thinkers capable of solving problems together.

A LEARNING COMMUNITY OF TEACHERS (COHORT GROUPS . . . FOOD MATTERS)

In an old school building in the Pasadena Unified School District, 15 teachers, representing different grades and subjects and different types of learners, hiked up steep stairs carrying their computers and books to Leakana Nhem's second-floor classroom.

They were the 18th cohort group of teachers to experience Design-Based Learning through Cal Poly's two-year master's degree program or one-year Certificate program. Each cohort selected a place for its weekly four-hour evening class meetings. These teachers had chosen Leakana's classroom because she had led the five-day Design-Based Learning Summer Institute for K-12 teachers at ArtCenter, the 40 contact hours that qualified as the first class in both the MA and Certificate programs. They wanted to see how a seasoned Design-Based Learning teacher organized a classroom to apply my methodology over an extended period of time, and to better understand why they hadn't been divided into a cohort group by grade level.

Drifting into the classroom on this Tuesday evening, weary after a day of teaching, the group chatted about traffic, the "horrors" of the day with students, about the lack of support from administrators, and about the agony of paperwork their district was requiring. They were hungry, looking forward to their potluck dinner.

High school Special Education Science teacher Lindsay Downs's concerns about presenting **BIG TOPIC** Design Challenges the "right way" spilled out into the conversation about food and traffic. At that time, she was a traditional teacher, anxious about Design-Based Learning and reluctant to bring it into her classroom until she totally understood the methodology. She had never taught problem solving to her Science students with learning disabilities, she said, and she was certain she would make mistakes.

Lindsay compared notes with pre-K teacher Susana Belmar (the only pre-K teacher in the master's program), whose teaching style, like Lindsay's, was traditionally formal. Susana's 3- and 4-year-old students sat in straight rows and she would tell them what to do before they tried to solve problems on their own. Sipping coffee, waiting for the rest of the cohort to arrive, these two teachers were joined by a kindergarten teacher who was struggling with similar issues. They began discussing ways they could change their classroom practice (ultimately, they did).

Instruction began as teachers presented a read-around and discussion of the required documentation of what had happened in their classrooms during a Design Challenge. The teachers described the steps of their process—including the sequential back-and-forth between what they did and what their students did. They humorously called this shared experience their "grueling struggle."

One teacher wrote about using the required Criteria List as a rubric for grading her students. Others questioned the validity of doing that, worrying that it could stop the flow of creativity. (This group added the third column to the "Don't Wants" and "Needs" of the Criteria List and called it "Points," to have a way to assess student achievement during a Design Challenge. This is now common practice in all trainings in the Design-Based Learning methodology.)

After a break for potluck dinner, the group was ready to "play," and play we did. On a large table, I laid out pieces of Styrofoam to be a landsite for a small City based on an existing location, asking them to imagine they were students about to build a City in the classroom. At first, the middle school History teacher, whose students were studying Ancient Rome, and the high school Chemistry teacher, whose students were learning about molecules, didn't see the significance of basing a Never-Before-Seen City on an actual location. I reminded them that it was to ground the "play" in reality as a visual cue for teaching the higher-level thinking skills associated with the parallel thinking of Non-Specific Transfer of Learning among academic subjects. I said a City in their own classroom can represent any location or system anywhere, as long as it has real-world constraints.

On we went, reading a map, choosing a location in Pasadena, parceling out individual pieces of property. The next half hour was spent on the Design Challenge of building a Never-Before-Seen Starter City **(BIG TOPIC: COMMUNITY)**. I pretended to be Mother Nature, causing problems in the City—a flood, a snowstorm—that the teachers needed to solve.

The teachers then named Guided Lessons (**small topics**) related to this Design Challenge. They wrote the lessons on color-coded Post-it Notes, dropping them into individual 3D Red Triangles representing the Design Challenge (see Chapter 4). As an exercise in reinforcing cross-curricular teaching, each teacher pulled out a Guided Lesson from someone else's 3D Red Triangle, read it aloud, and explained how it could apply to his or her own grade level.

The 3rd-grade teacher liked the kindergarten teacher's idea of having her students learn the concept of small-to-large by lining up Never-Before-Seen Buildings according to size. He said that he could also do that and have his 3rd graders measure and compare the size of their buildings to teach them about volume, ratio, and proportion. The high school Math teacher expanded the possibilities, saying that she could have her students solve equations based on the buildings' assigned mass. The common wisdom is that kindergarten teachers have nothing to learn from being with high school teachers and vice versa, and most planning sessions in schools take place at grade level, or in like subject matter meetings.

When I began working with cohort groups of K–12 teachers, they didn't have much to say to each other when they arrived. They were hesitant to offer feedback when listening to how others practiced Design-Based Learning at their various grade levels. One evening, thinking that a more social atmosphere would help, I had brought dinner. It did the trick. Having the time to vent while sharing a convivial meal energized the teachers and they bonded as collaborators, willing to learn from each other.

Our dinners became potlucks. One teacher loved to bake and had a surprise for her group every week. Sometimes the food was elaborate, with salads, main dishes, and desserts. One teacher celebrated his birthday by cooking an entire dinner for everyone, right down to baking his birthday cake.

When teachers feel more comfortable offering constructive comments on each other's classroom documentation as peer reviewers, they ask good questions and write considered observations. They have fun urging each other to use more descriptive language and to provide more detail about any problems they encounter. They ask each other how they relate their required Guided Lessons to their **BIG TOPIC** Design Challenges, and how they assess their students' achievements.

They look forward to reading comments by their peers and trainers. Teachers' innate creativity spills out all over their writing and their classroom practice.

In a safe, supportive environment, teachers feel free to examine their classroom practice. Their candid flow of ideas about how to meet the education code requirements and weave them into my Design-Based Learning methodology shows the versatility of teaching creative thinking and cultivating students' curiosity to deliver subject matter.

THE IMPORTANCE OF "WHY"

In 1970, my 5th and 6th graders decided to go on strike against me . . . for giving them too much homework. I had just returned to the classroom from the five-week Los Angeles Unified School District teachers strike. I had spent the mornings on the picket line and the afternoons with my team-teaching partner, Ruth Glatt, teaching our combined classes of 3rd–6th-grade underserved students in some of their homes—at the invitation of their parents—and taking them on public buses to museums and events, including the first Earth Day celebration, held at UCLA. (You couldn't do any of this today.)

I forced myself to listen calmly to my students' complaints. I asked them if they knew why I gave them homework, and the response was, "No, why *do* we have to do it?" I grabbed the book of state-mandated teaching requirements, showing the students that I had to assign at least 30 minutes of homework daily. Accepting that there was indeed a "why," and that it was not arbitrary on my part, my students asked if they could invent their own homework, so long as I approved it. Since most of them, up to this point, had rarely turned in any homework at all, I agreed. My criteria were that they had to spend the prescribed amount of time and write a minimum of one page describing what they did. Some of the kids thought they had put one over on me, but no matter what they did, or how mundane, I always got at least one page of detailed and descriptive writing from each of them. From then on, it was homework without complaint.

Over time, my students' self-imposed homework assignments became more and more sophisticated. Their choice of assignments and their writing improved dramatically and their Language Arts test scores soared. Ten-year-old Jack, who was a member of the Winnebago Nation, wrote that he sat for 20 minutes looking at a tree and turned in an original two-page poem about his experience.

The significance of questioning in the teaching process began to gel for me and "why" became my go-to word, even for something as simple as a piece of trash on the floor. Rather than ordering a student to pick it up, I took a few seconds of class time to ask why it should be picked up. ("Someone might slip on it." "It doesn't look nice.") After that, my students noticed when something was on the floor and automatically picked it up. Their attention to small things out of order in the classroom led them to propose solutions to how supplies and books could be stored more efficiently, how the classroom furniture could be rearranged so that everyone could see each other and me, and how they could keep their small City clean and organized. Classroom management became a partnership.

This occurred during the 1969–1970 school year, when I was piloting my Design-Based Learning methodology, team-teaching with 3rd- and 4th-grade teacher Ruth Glatt (see Chapter 2). Our endless hours of talking about "why" had spilled into our daily classroom practice.

Asking students "why" was something I did (and still do) so easily, but when I began teaching teachers, I had trouble convincing them it was important. Leslie Stoltz, who graduated in the master's program in 1998 and taught teachers with me, showed me her approach to asking "why" questions. When teachers would describe completely frontloading a Design Challenge, rather than coming at it backwards, I was frustrated that they didn't see their mistake. I wanted to jump in and tell them what they were doing wrong, but Leslie would calmly ask the whole group what they thought and why, modeling what they were to do with their own students.

In one cohort group, kindergarten teacher Karen told about giving her students a Design Challenge to tell something special about themselves in a Never-Before-Seen Introduction (**BIG TOPIC: IDENTITY**). They were to choose an object that they could hold in their hand and that would explain something they liked about themselves. Worried that her students were too young to understand that one thing could stand in for another, Karen picked up a doll and rocked it in her arms, telling her students that something special about her was that she liked babies and that was why she chose a doll as her object. Every student in the class selected a doll as their object.

Karen came to class, asking what she had done wrong. With Leslie's patient guidance, the other teachers in the cohort group asked Karen why she thought her students had copied her. She said, "Oh, my god, everything I did asked them to imitate me, even when I asked for an original, Never-Before-Seen Introduction. What I wanted was for them to think creatively and to learn to question their choices."

Teachers who ask their students "why" and *wait for the answer*, lead students to open up in that silent space and give voice to their thinking.

Perhaps it is because I am the granddaughter of a Talmudic scholar that I assume everyone is always asking "What do you think and why?" As I look back on all my years of teaching teachers, my relentless probing for answers is probably what kept them with me, even if I was sometimes impatient and wanted to give my answer instead of listening to theirs—exactly what I was asking them not to do with their students.

Some seasoned K–12 teachers know about tricking students into learning. Some say that they already do projects with their students that are similar to Design Challenges and that they are put off by having to constantly tell their students to consider the "why" integral to every Design Challenge. Their hesitation disappears once they see their students engaged in creative thinking.

The "why" process in Design-Based Learning is taught throughout the methodology's 6½ Steps of Backwards Thinking™. When students design three-dimensional, Never-Before-Seen answers to a curriculum-related dilemma, the teacher uses their built artifacts to ask questions that connect "why" with creative thinking: "You made a light bulb, but light bulbs already exist. Why is yours different?"

"Why" students every step of the way, conveying interest and respect, not accusation, and engagement happens automatically.

CHAPTER
16

TRUST

The campus of El Segundo Elementary School in the Compton Unified School District in Los Angeles was a chaotic environment when I arrived there in 1974. It was troubled by random shootings, gang violence, and constant fights on the playground. Funded by a grant from the U.S. Office of Education, I had agreed to train teachers in my Design-Based Learning methodology (then known as City Building Education) at the school. To ensure success, Emma Hulett, El Segundo's principal, had selected a dozen of her 45 teachers whom she thought would be most willing to participate in a six-week summer training program involving teachers, kids, and university architecture students.

Emma understood the value of building a tabletop City in the classroom as a dynamic metaphor pertaining to any grade level and subject area. She wasn't worried that students who built a City in the 3rd grade would get bored building a City in the 4th, 5th, and 6th grades. Her teachers took more convincing.

I was often impatient with what I saw as their lack of understanding and would go to Emma's office after training sessions to vent about them. (Emma, a magnificent leader, listened patiently to teachers complaining about me, too.) Three years into our work together, I was complaining yet again, when Emma closed the door to her office, looked me straight in the eye, and said, "Doreen, any methodology that lets kids fail, has to let teachers fail." Emma reminded me that I had deliberately planned for "mistakes" to be an integral part of my methodology to teach students to identify dilemmas, ask why, and find new solutions through Design Challenges, research, and revisions.

Emma's reminder was a wake-up call, and not the last I would need over the years I spent refining my process of teaching teachers.

Many of Emma's teachers continued using my methodology in their classrooms for years after the grant funding ended. They reported that their students excelled and behavioral issues diminished. Conflicts tended to be disagreements over what the students felt they should build for their City. I witnessed the students' enthusiasm for learning in a big way when nine classrooms put their Cities together outdoors, after the university architecture students funded by the grant took them through a meticulous revision process. Surprise: all of the Cities and their pathways fitted together. On their own, these students had communicated from one classroom to another to make that happen.

During my four years at El Segundo Elementary School, I refined the model for training teachers that I had developed at the Smithsonian Institution in 1972. Although my experience in Compton was sometimes fraught and often frustrating for everyone, what kept me there was my respect for the students, for the teachers—who wanted a better way to engage their students—and for Emma, who persevered in leading her teachers to redefine their teaching practice.

My experience in Compton was on my mind when the master's degree emphasis in Design-Based Learning began at Cal Poly Pomona in 1995, but I was too intimidated by the "convince me" attitude of teachers in the early cohort groups to act on Emma Hulett's plea to trust teachers to "get it." I felt that I had to beg teachers to think about what seemed obvious to me. I didn't always practice my own methodology's teaching technique by asking them, "What do you think about that and why?" so they would learn to present their solutions, advocate for their own ideas, and compromise, just as their own students would.

If a teacher said how much her students loved building their City, but that it was messy, that it took too much time away from teaching, and was it okay to omit the building part, I would point out why making things in a context was necessary and didn't they see that serious teaching required "play" and finessing students into learning?

As teachers built artifacts to solve a Design Challenge that I gave them, I would sometimes cut the process short, lecturing about what was being done and why. When I had them put a City together, knowing their land pieces wouldn't fit—roads wouldn't connect or would run into doorways—instead of trusting them to absorb and discuss this planned "mistake," I would often jump the gun and tell them I did it on purpose and that they should do the same and ask their students to figure it out.

In those moments, I became the "sage on the stage," sabotaging the philosophical foundation of my methodology: that there are no wrong answers in the deliberate "play" of Design-Based Learning, as long as a solution to a Design Challenge can be justified. I had to learn to listen and wait. I had to trust teachers to creatively think through their own solutions.

It took 10 years and 10 cohort groups of teachers after the master's program began for me to feel that I had reached what author/journalist Malcolm Gladwell called the "point of mastery." I finally felt comfortable asking teachers to experience Design-Based Learning as their students would. I began bringing in tons of my "picture" books on art, poetry, and science to talk about how each artist, architect, scientist, or clothing designer changed the way people looked at things. Teachers came to class to see what crazy thing I would present, and we enjoyed arguing about the validity of my selection of talent. Many from this group have continued practicing my methodology in their classrooms and have trained other teachers.

I can only assume that teachers who have put up with me at my frustrated worst through the years could tell that I was sincere in asking them to do what was best for their students. The widespread acceptance of my Design-Based Learning methodology enabled me to see that I could do with teachers what I did so easily with my own students when I piloted my methodology: trust them to make original designs, to explain the "why" of their thinking, to seek out better answers and better questions, to collaborate as a group, and to make subject matter connections across the curriculum.

Developing a Design-Based Learning Classroom

To be serious about preparing students for their futures, the culture of the classroom has to mirror aspects of life outside the classroom. In the Design-Based Learning methodology, a student-built, tabletop City and the classroom itself become student-centered micro worlds, parallel hubs of active student participation.

As they build their City (always based on an actual location), students are taught real-world decision-making skills. These skills can be reinforced by having students learn to compare the functioning of their City to the functioning of their classroom. In this back-and-forth flow of Non-Specific Transfer of Learning, between their roles in the City and in the classroom, they learn how subject matter can have multiple applications.

Ten years into my teaching career, when I first ventured into having my elementary school students roughly build a City in my classroom in the 1969–1970 school year (see Chapter 2), I asked them if they wanted to run it as if they lived there. They jumped at the chance to be in charge and their eagerness to learn about government and civic responsibility enabled me to teach those subjects far beyond what was required at their grade level. I had them role-play as citizens of their City and choose volunteers for leadership positions. While they grappled with complex issues about governance of their City and wrote descriptions of the jobs needed to make it work, I taught them to make comparisons between their roles in the City and the classroom.

To teach my students how to manage their City and the classroom, and to give everyone a job, I divided the City and the physical classroom into the same five Council Districts. I had the "citizens" in each District elect a Council representative and an alternate in case of absence. I had them research the jobs in an actual city and different types of governments. I guided them to select a democratic government for their City. I made a chart of their government structure, taught them to conduct meetings and how to make and follow simple agendas, and to plan, record, and evaluate required tasks.

Things took off when I had them invent parallel jobs in the classroom and "apply" for a job of their choice. I asked the Mayor of the City to call the class to order. I had the Commissioner of Housing work with his committee to make certain that the desks were orderly inside and out. The City's Commissioner of Recreation and her committee were in charge of distributing and storing playground equipment. I showed the City Clerk my own daily teaching agendas and I taught her how to make separate agendas for meetings about the City and the classroom. I had her keep a list of lessons accomplished each day in the classroom and make a log of events in the City. I kept this City and classroom governance going because my problems with a messy classroom and bad behavior stopped.

The leaders of the Council Districts met with their citizens to identify problems in the City (pollution, for example) and what a counterpart might be in the classroom (messiness). I taught them to post advance notices on the bulletin board saying when City Meetings would take place and how long they would last. The students worked together to decide how to revise the City to solve the problems they identified. They learned and practiced the skills for making oral presentations and for listening and questioning. After approval from their committees and the Mayor, they proceeded with their plans. They couldn't wait to "fix" things.

One of the problems the students identified was the construction of City Hall, built by Portia. The Housing Commission's Building Inspectors said it didn't meet their criteria. At a City Meeting, the other "citizens" voted unanimously to reject Portia's three-story creation, pointing out that it would be dark inside because there were no windows. (The class knew that windows and skylights brought light into buildings. I had recently had Ralph Knowles, an American Institute of Architects gold medalist and a USC professor, come to class to speak with them on the subject.) Portia disagreed with her classmates' criticism of her craftsmanship.

I was ready to step in and stop the agony if it went too far, but I felt that learning about democracy required experience with the democratic process, which is not always smooth! Instead of putting my arm around Portia and scolding the other kids for making her feel bad, I met with the Building Inspectors and had them review their decision and practice how to write a letter to Portia politely explaining why the building was unacceptable.

After hearing from her peers in a kinder, gentler way, Portia redesigned her building to meet the requirements set by the Building Inspectors. She received high praise from the whole class for her outstanding effort—to such a degree that, when election time rolled around, Portia was voted Mayor of the City and she became the leader of the classroom.

I didn't let the students think that because they held positions of authority in their City and classroom government, they could do whatever they wanted. I taught them manners, protocol, and even went over "Robert's Rules of Order" with them. I required that they schedule a time limit for each item to be discussed, and had them present the agenda to me for final approval. They responded to this structure and learned to adhere to the rules while running their meetings.

In a Design-Based Learning classroom, as students build and run a City and use what they learn through Guided Lessons, shared decision-making becomes organic, coordinated, and facilitated by the teacher. Students role-play to learn about the process of governance, internalizing and applying what they learn as they present and vote on rules and regulations. They learn to seek information from multiple resources, document their experience, give presentations, and to collaborate, working together and with their teacher. The result: a student-centered classroom. (Although teachers of single subjects are not required to teach about government, setting up a government structure for the City enhances classroom management and increases student buy-in to subject matter.)

17

ORGANIC CLASSROOM
MANAGEMENT AND
GOVERNANCE

The "City" and the Classroom
as Micro Worlds

*Our new City government is cool because it feels like we are doing the real
world in school.*

—Jin Ko Zheng, 4th-grade student,
San Gabriel Unified School District

Setting up and refining the Starter City, students learn about the structure of governance and how to make democratic decisions and laws that shape their built environment. Those laws, the rights of people, the pros and cons of environmental issues, the height limitation on buildings, the appropriate energy systems, and the solutions to human problems are decided and communicated, and come into being.

A system of governance in the Never-Before-Seen Starter City provides a framework for resolving the problems that arise as the City evolves.

Students learn to manage the City by assuming roles as government leaders. An organizational structure with steps for accomplishing tasks teaches students to present their designs for the City, give and receive feedback, and ask "why" questions, to gain understanding of ways to organize. This process is called decentralization or division of labor. As a Starter City is revised and students practice leadership and management skills, the government of the City becomes increasingly more fluid.

To run the City government, students learn to develop "public policy" and ways to make it work by defining group wishes and how to modify and implement them. To regulate the governance of the Starter City, a series of curriculum-based Guided Lessons from selected **BIG TOPICS**, are taught through the course of a semester or school year.

These **BIG TOPICS** may include:

- **ORGANIZATION**
  Organization develops for a purpose

- **REPRESENTATION**
  Representative government empowers individuals to do things in the best interest of the group and is accountable to the people it represents

- **REGULATION AND ENFORCEMENT**
  All forms of organization regulate behavior, with rules and regulations or laws and a system of enforcement

- **LEADERSHIP**
  Leaders can be chosen and maintained in a variety of ways

- **ADAPTABILITY**
  People invent the city and they can adapt and transform it

- **INTERCONNECTEDNESS**
  The whole is greater than the sum of its parts

- **CONSISTENCY**
  A defined routine achieves continuity

Refining the Starter City enables the students as planners to consciously try an organizational structure with a method for resolving differences. Roles change and students investigate the nature of government organizations, why laws are created, the consequences of their designs, and the constraints of the effectiveness of their designs. If these turn out to be flawed, policymaking techniques are used as the basis for revision.

Practice with the democratic process is difficult; the back-and-forth communication between the large group and the small group is often frustrating. Once the laws have been established, written down, and made accessible, students begin to role-play government positions, and decide on penalties, sanctions, and other methods of enforcing the codes, as well as ways of resolving disputes.

> At first, I didn't see the point of all the government activities. I see now how much learning, especially in terms of respect and responsibility, will come from it. I learned that the less I force collaboration and the more I shut up and step back, the more my students learn to collaborate.
> —Natalie Bezdjian, kindergarten teacher, Rose & Alex
> Pilibos Armenian School, Hollywood, California

ROLE-PLAYING

> What I like about my new City government is that they're acting like it is real. They're not playing around.
> —Bailey Mattocks, 4th-grade student,
> San Gabriel Unified School District

In the Design-Based Learning, Backwards Thinking™ methodology, teaching students to make comparisons between the organization and the functioning of their City and classroom is the key to Non-Specific Transfer of Learning. The City is a "near" experience because it belongs to the students, providing a context for them to learn decision-making skills and to see the effectiveness of their decisions in miniature. The classroom is a "far" experience and usually belongs to the teacher. To learn to use "near" information (the City) and apply it to "far" information (the classroom), students begin by identifying the jobs needed to run their City. They are taught to role-play those jobs as they make decisions about how their Starter City will evolve.

Non-Specific Transfer of Learning—reusable learning—occurs as students learn to identify the similarities and differences between their City jobs and jobs in the classroom: Mayor/class president, Head of Parks and Recreation/ball monitor, Building Inspector/desk monitor (because the desk houses students' work), Health Inspector/student in charge of the first-aid kit, Transportation Commissioner/student coordinating movement around and out of the classroom, Utilities Commissioner/student in charge of the pencil sharpener, the lights, paper supplies, and distributing computers. Some jobs can even be made up.

Through Guided Lessons, with a teacher-made organizational chart listing parallel structure and job descriptions as a prompt, students learn to speak about or write descriptions of jobs they want in their City and how those jobs compare to jobs in the classroom. They learn how those jobs work in a real city by listening to their teacher describe the jobs or by doing their own research. Some teachers have their students campaign for the jobs of their choice in the City by giving speeches, writing applications, and designing self-promotional products.

To lock Non-Specific Transfer of Learning into students' big muscles, some teachers have them make small, wearable Never-Before-Seen Objects that are reversible in order to display both job functions. In practice, as they role-play, students wear their Objects with pride of ownership in their City and classroom jobs (and they invariably notice when one of their peers wears an Object the wrong way round).

This supervised role-playing achieves Non-Specific Transfer of Learning, teaching students that a concept taught in one setting can be applied in a variety of settings.

(Students learned that one job is like the other, but not the same, in ESL teacher Annette Dellemonico's class at Sepulveda Middle School in the Los Angeles Unified School District. Annette had class officers make reversible paper sashes naming their classroom jobs in one color on one side and corresponding jobs in their small Paradise Hills City in another color on the other side. The students reversed their sashes depending on whether they were having a class meeting or a Paradise Hills meeting.)

When I started teaching teachers to include dual role-playing in their Guided Lessons, they were hesitant until they found that when students took on these transferable City and classroom jobs, less time was spent on classroom management and discipline. Even when a problem arose, like messy desks or an untidy City, students understood why someone had to be in charge.

Elementary school teachers adopt this kind of role-playing easily. High school and middle school teachers may say that they can't take time away from their subject matter. When secondary teachers do involve their students in daily classroom management mirroring the governing of the built City, they see how much more receptive the students are to academic learning.

One middle school Math teacher had students compute the time that City and classroom meetings took. An Art teacher had students create election posters and nameplates for their jobs and a template for a meeting agenda. A Science teacher had students select scientific topics related to the City and to the school garden for discussion at their meetings.

In what appeared at first to be an impossible situation, a high school Math teacher in the Design-Based Learning master's degree program, working with students with severe behavioral problems, struggled to connect the City and classroom governments. Looking for ways to integrate Math and government, the teacher began setting weekly 5- to 10-minute City and classroom meetings, increasing the number of meetings as more possibilities for teaching Math arose. His students used the government rules and regulations that they themselves established to get everything from classwork to homework done on time. The teacher set up a timekeeping system to teach the students how to use percentages and graphs to portray the time devoted to anything: students coming to class late, the length of a meeting, who participated, and how long to discuss City or classroom problems. After a few weeks, the students' behavior improved significantly and the teacher was better able to teach Math topics.

The following chart shows possible parallel structures for job-related role-playing, clarifying the comparisons among a real city, a classroom, and a school.

COMPARATIVE VOCABULARY OF THE CITY, CLASSROOM, AND SCHOOL			
Categories of City Commissions or Departments	City Components	Classroom Comparisons	School Comparisons
Housing	Private homes	Desks, chairs, bins	Classrooms
Movement/ Transportation	Streets, roads, Freeway ramps	Paths, aisles Front door	Hallways
Government facilities	Civic Center City Hall	Front black-board Teacher's desk	Main Office Community Room

Categories of City Commissions or Departments	City Components	Classroom Comparisons	School Comparisons
Cultural facilities	Museums Theaters Concert venues Art galleries	Display areas Art supplies Instruments	Auditorium Music Room
Education	Libraries Educational facilities	Bookcases The classroom	School Library Whole facility
Medical facilities and services	Hospitals	Emergency supplies	Nurse's Office
Recreational facilities	Parks Entertainment venues	Playground supplies	Playground
Religious facilities	Places of worship Cemeteries	Flag Storage file drawers	
Public Utilities and Services	Energy Water Disposal systems	Light switches Sink Wastebasket Pencil sharpener	Bathrooms Drinking fountains Custodial facility Storage
Industry	Factories		Maker spaces

Categories of City Commissions or Departments	City Components	Classroom Comparisons	School Comparisons
Commercial facilities	Shopping centers Banks	Storage Supplies Equipment	Cafeteria
Open Space	Space between buildings	Space between desks	Space between classrooms
Boundaries	City limits	Walls	Fence

Post-it Ville (Parallel Learning)

The playful Post-it Ville activity puts learning about role comparisons into students' big muscles. Using the Comparative Vocabulary Chart, students assume the roles of a specific City commission or department and choose Post-it Notes in a specific color to represent their jobs. They move around the classroom, sticking their color-coded Post-it Notes onto places and things that they think compare to components of the City. This activity demonstrates that there isn't just one answer for corresponding roles in the City and the classroom. What is "right" depends on how students justify a point of view as they define, speak about, and write about the comparisons they identify. (One class discussed how and why a file cabinet in the classroom could be a cemetery or a jail.)

City Components	Classroom Comparisons	Color
Private homes	Desks, chairs, bins	Light yellow
Streets, roads, freeway ramps	Paths, aisles, front door	Hot pink

City Components	Classroom Comparisons	Color
Civic Center City Hall	Front blackboard Teacher's desk	Purple
Museums Theaters Concert venues Art galleries	Display areas Art supplies Instruments	Teal green
Libraries Educational facilities	Bookcases The classroom	Light pink
Hospitals	Emergency supplies	Green
Parks Entertainment venues	Playground supplies	French blue
Places of worship Cemeteries	Flag Storage file drawers Wastebasket	Neon yellow
Energy Water Disposal systems	Light switches Sink Wastebasket Pencil sharpener	Blue
Factories		Orange
Shopping centers Banks	Storage Supplies Equipment	Medium pink
Space between buildings	Space between desks	White

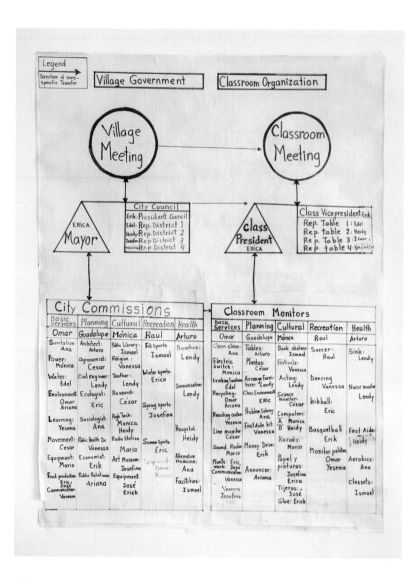

To promote his 2nd graders' independence, Miguel Fernandez had his students refer to this chart (above) to keep track of their dual jobs in their City, "The Village," and in the classroom. When visitors came to Miguel's classroom in the Pomona Unified School District, his students gave them a tour, proudly explaining their corresponding jobs. (One of Miguel's most demanding students, who was in charge of

Cultivating Curiosity

storage, had decided on his own to inventory everything in the class-room closets and even devised a check-out list to keep track of con-sumable and nonconsumable supplies.)

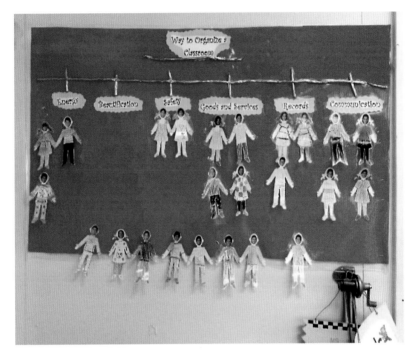

Third-grade teacher Norma Juarez's organizational chart (above) showing her students' City and classroom jobs at San Jose Elementary and Highly Gifted Magnet School in Mission Hills, Los Angeles Unified School District.

MOVING THE FURNITURE

"Come to my house after school," I'd say when I was a kid to any stu-dent that I thought needed help with learning. This started when I was in the 2nd grade in my mixed neighborhood in Toronto, Canada. I would invite what would now be called "underserved" students to my house, giving them snacks and teaching them skills that they were finding difficult to grasp in school. We "played" school, sitting on chairs in a circle doing word problems in math and reading out loud. The time I spent with them gave purpose to my day, taking me into a world where I had fun (and away from the drama of my family).

I was always "teacher's pet" and my 3rd-grade teacher, Miss Mac-Millan, was my role model for what a teacher should be. My passion for learning caught fire when we studied China. We gathered around her at the front of the room, away from our rigid desks that were bolted to the floor, to make and drink Chinese tea. I was spellbound. The classroom changed, softened, and became China for that moment.

That childhood memory of making something tactile and changing my perspective of the physical classroom environment led me years later to do research about hands-on learning and the relationship between the placement of furniture in the classroom and learning. In the early twentieth century, the simple act of unbolting classroom desks from the floor expanded the possibilities for learning through doing. This turned out to be one of the most profound changes in American education.

Perhaps it was my dad, too, who influenced me. He had a quirky habit of rearranging the furniture in our house and I always looked forward to the unexpected changes. I thought my mother was right when, each time, she jokingly said that a map to find our way around would help.

When I started teaching, I often rearranged my classroom. My students reacted to each change, demanding that I explain why I did it and offering their own ideas. After many years of being in charge of these arrangements, I recognized that my students wanted me to hear their opinions about reorganizing the classroom. Listening to them justify their opinions turned out to be a learning gold mine.

Elementary school teachers teach all or most subjects to the same 25–35 students all day long. Middle school and high school teachers have rotating groups of 100 or more students in each of their specialized subject areas. Managing all of this, while attempting to develop a student-centered classroom, is difficult. Having students learn to make decisions about where the classroom furniture goes (to accommodate a tabletop City and to organize and store things) can be a catalyst for activating the City and classroom governments. This activity integrates the intentional teaching of management and civic responsibility into any required curriculum.

In a Design-Based Learning student-centered classroom, students name and categorize places with different functions in the City and the classroom, practicing the thinking skills necessary for organizing the social and physical structures of each. Working in their government groups, students discuss such questions as: What is a classroom for and why does it look the way it does? What are the good and bad aspects of the current classroom organization and why? What can be changed, moved, installed, removed, and why? How are changes limited by fire and safety regulations, teacher requirements, and costs? Who owns the furniture? Who owns the classroom? Who/what is the Board of Education?

When I taught elementary school and a project involved moving desks around or working outdoors for a short time, students who would otherwise gobble up my time were too engaged to cause disruptions. I used the categorical placement of things in the classroom as a teaching tool (and even once, for a few hours, I let my students try out some of their own classroom designs). Everything improved: their thinking, their ability to justify their ideas for rearranging the furniture—and my classroom management. After almost 10 years of K–12 teaching, I was systematically having my students decide where the desks should go and why. My desk eventually left the room entirely and I simply parked my materials either on a table or in a closet. It was unexpectedly liberating.

For many years, when teaching teachers, I asked them to do what I had done. I had them research the benefits of a physically structured, student-centered classroom. (Hardly a new idea. In ancient Greece, students sat in a circle while engaging in contemplative discussions and thought.) Teachers recognize the value of using the physical classroom to teach decision-making and critical thinking, but may hesitate to bring about a student-driven physical change in their own classrooms. They rightfully worry that their students won't like thinking about where things go, that administrators will complain that governance lessons are time off-task from the mandated curriculum, and that the classroom will be a mess.

That may happen initially, but the results of teaching higher-level thinking skills in this fundamentally organic way make those concerns a nonissue.

CLASSROOM-IN-A-BAG

In Design-Based Learning trainings, to promote a student-centered classroom, teachers of all grade levels and subject areas learn to teach their students that the arrangement of furniture informs the functionality of a physical space anywhere.

I give the teachers a brown paper grocery bag with the top folded down (a shoebox works, too) to represent a rough scale model of their classroom. I then have them do what they will teach their students to do: fashion the main elements of their classroom's interior (from cardboard, paper, clay, or found materials) and position these elements in the bag, including space for the student-built City. Then, using the same elements and adding new ones, they generate a unique but workable classroom. They present their plans to their peers, give and get feedback to see if they met the preset criteria, evaluate and revise their plans, and document their steps in writing—required skills in all subjects.

Back in their classrooms, some teachers set aside short periods of time for their students to test various plans for the classroom reorganization, asking "why" questions as students discuss and justify their ideas. The more that students rearrange the furniture and fixtures in their Classroom-in-a-Bag and learn to discuss the effects of their changes (often finding things are out of scale and they have forgotten to include the classroom clock, the flag, the teacher's desk, or even the door to the classroom), the better for teaching critical thinking and decision-making and achieving a student-centered classroom.

A three-dimensional model makes visible the information that would not be apparent in a two-dimensional floor plan. In a three-dimensional model, the space underneath tables, for example, can be imagined as storage space. Teachers have students put their plans into action in the physical classroom, guiding the process by asking them "why" every step of the way. Many teachers repeat Classroom-in-a-Bag reorganization over and over throughout the school year in response to changing needs.

Richard Rosa, who taught high school Science in Pasadena, California, connected Classroom-in-a-Bag to teaching the scientific method of testing hypotheses. His students didn't grasp the meaning of the word until this hands-on, reorganization analogy taught them to think like scientists. Referring to Richard's Criteria List, the students mapped and labeled the classroom, discussed their hypotheses for making changes, then tested the validity of their hypotheses by physically rearranging the classroom.

When a large group of visitors arrived to observe Richard's Design-Based Learning classroom, his high school seniors knew where everything was and why. They were so articulate and enthusiastic as they conducted a tour of their classroom arrangement that one visitor was moved to ask how many were planning to go to college. *All* of the students' hands went up.

"I had asked these same students this question on the first day of class," Richard said later. "At that time, fewer than a fourth of my students thought that college was within their reach."

A STUDENT-CENTERED CLASSROOM

2nd Grade

Marlyn Burleigh Silver and Cindy Gedgaudas, teachers in Sulphur Springs Union School District in Saugus, were not timid in teaching their 2nd graders about classroom reorganization. They had an architect-in-residence student make a furnished scale model of their classroom. Adhering to Marlyn and Cindy's Criteria List, the students worked in groups, rearranging the miniature furniture in the model to come up with and draw plans to reorganize their classroom. They justified every placement in the plans they drew.

Once the groups presented their plans, Marlyn and Cindy took the plunge. They let the students test out their plans, group by group, by rearranging the classroom their way and having everyone live in it for one school day, then evaluating how it worked. As Guided Lessons during the process, which took a few hours over five school days, the students learned how to read and make clear floor plans that they derived from the scale model. Through other Guided Lessons, they learned about directionality, scale, and the higher-level thinking skills associated with communication and decision-making as they justified the function and placement of things.

The students were so engaged with this short-lived exercise that they wanted to give up recess to do it. Most of the rearranged desks stayed in place an hour or less as students identified all kinds of problems with their plans. The winning group, by unanimous student vote, arranged all of the desks in a big circle so that everyone could see everyone else. Marlyn and Cindy, initially dubious about this arrangement, discovered that participation in group discussions soared, and they kept the arrangement in place for several days—until the custodian, not having been told that this was a significant learning experience and would not last forever, charged into the room, complaining that he wasn't going to be able to clean the classroom anymore because he had to move the tables each night to get into the center of the circle. The students were disappointed, but understood why their favorite plan wouldn't work. They learned that practical concerns mattered and that what worked in a small-scale model, might not work big. To solve the problem, they figured out how to modify their circle arrangement so the custodian would have access to the center of the room.

Although, due to the size of the two combined classes, the circle arrangement proved impractical in the long run, Marlyn and Cindy's students now saw themselves not only as problem finders, but as problem solvers.

Kindergarten

Jane Devlin, a veteran teacher in the Pasadena Unified School District, was uneasy when she began the master's degree program in Design-Based Learning at Cal Poly in 2011. She wondered if the methodology would prove to be beyond her kindergartners' capabilities when she put them in charge of numerous tasks: keeping the line quiet in the hallways, taking the attendance folder to the office, distributing and gathering up class work, watering the class garden, seeing that the classroom was clean at the end of the day, and governing "Sierra Niños," the City they were building. "I was sure that they would not do these things properly, and I was right," Jane said. "There were problems and messes. Students argued and tattled."

Jane persevered, reviewing job requirements with her students and demonstrating how to do the jobs properly. "To my surprise, the children began to absorb the information," she said. "In our daily, five-minute classroom meetings, they identified problems and suggested solutions that were voted on by all. The solutions they implemented didn't always work, but when they failed, I learned to give them time to discuss why, and to come up with alternatives."

The critical teaching moment occurred when Jane's kindergartners came up with a three-dimensional, Never-Before-Seen Solution as a reminder to walk quietly in line together. They proposed holding onto a rope every time they lined up. Jane said that she had to use great restraint to keep from interfering with this absurd suggestion and pointing out that hanging onto a rope in the hallway could be a safety hazard. (She was also worried about the reaction from her administrators.)

"I wanted my students to discover for themselves, with my super-vision, why the rope was a bad idea," she said, "and they did. They found the rope was cumbersome, it got shut in the doors, and on the stairs it was difficult to hold onto. They hastily voted the rope out of use and discussed new solutions.

"These very young children grew to see themselves as important members of the classroom," Jane said. "And I had more energy and patience as their teacher. As time passed, my class had fewer behavior problems than others at my school. I can only conclude that this was because my students felt that they had some control over classroom governance."

Middle School (Math)

Sharon Soto, a Math teacher in the Rowland Unified School District, entered the master's degree program in Design-Based Learning in 2009. Applying the methodology, Sharon's middle school students built what they called "Math City" to learn Math.

Sharon formalized role-playing in both Math City and the classroom. Adhering to Sharon's rules and those of the school, her students made their own policy to create a classroom government. When classroom rules were violated, the students held five-minute meetings to identify the problem, review the data, and resolve the issue. They learned to assume responsibility for their own behavior. As a Guided Lesson, they researched, compiled, and compared the statistics of current behavior problems in class to those that had occurred before their classroom government was put in place.

In her master's project, Sharon documented that rather than feeling "like a dictator" patrolling her classroom to be sure that it was clean and quiet, her role changed from "sole disciplinarian to facilitator and mediator."

2nd Grade

When Josh Whittemore was a novice 2nd-grade teacher in the Rowland Unified School District, he was accustomed to doing most of the classroom jobs himself and having his students sit in straight rows while he taught. As a Design-Based Learning teacher, he experimented with desk placement and made room for the supplies used in the three-dimensional Design Challenges he gave his students as they built and ran their City, "Creatureville."

"When my students realized that the whole room was a place to create, not just a place to have right and wrong answers," Josh said, "it made the space conducive to learning. And when the room was student-centered, they became comfortable trying new things."

1st Grade

After some trial and error in introducing her students to Design-Based Learning, Eliza Ong, a then-1st-grade teacher in the Rowland Unified School District, rethought both her classroom environment and her teaching approach. Moving bookcases and desks, creating a more open and inviting library area, complete with pillows, Eliza made space for the "Better City" model her students were building. She designed a portable landsite by adding wheels to a 4 × 6½-foot wooden bed frame. Shifting the orientation of the classroom environment to reflect more of the students' thinking and learning, she posted student-made charts on the classroom's History Wall. With her guidance, these charts included a Criteria List with assessments for each Design Challenge.

"With their City in front of them, and their charts for easy reference," Eliza said, "the governance of my classroom changed greatly when I invited student discussions. Conquering my initial impulse to jump in and correct their mistakes, I learned to facilitate a process that would teach my 1st graders to find the right answers through discussion. With encouragement, my students no longer expected me to be the only one to identify problems and provide solutions."

Having her students analyze and address City and classroom situations taught them to be leaders, Eliza said. When a City or classroom problem arose, the 1st graders asked for a meeting to discuss it. "I found that even when I gave them time limits, my very young students could learn to resolve problems, make decisions, and become more independent thinkers," she said. (Eliza now teaches middle school and continues this process.)

2nd Grade

As a seasoned 2nd-grade teacher in the Pasadena Unified School District and a 1995 Teacher of Excellence Award recipient, Marta Rosales had always been comfortable deciding on classroom procedures, writing the rules, and selecting class monitors and helpers.

It wasn't until her second year of applying Design-Based Learning in her classroom and having her students build "Magic Land City," that Marta introduced division of labor and facilitated City and classroom meetings.

In her Design-Based Learning master's project, Marta described being apprehensive about delegating authority and that she intervened often during the first meetings. She would offer opinions or solutions, until her students began assuming roles in the City and the classroom, and she saw that both places became important to them.

As her students learned the process of self-governance, Marta had fewer behavior problems. She began interacting with them "at a different intellectual level," and "felt a sense of camaraderie with them, requesting their opinions about classroom procedures and events." She was more trusting that her students would make good choices about their City and classroom management because she had given them the tools to do so. Voting became part of decision-making in her classroom.

Marta changed her classroom environment by moving her desk to a corner and placing the student-built "Magic Land City" in the center of the room to emphasize its significance as a major context for cross-curricular learning. She arranged students' desks in clusters around "Magic Land." Grouping the desks encouraged cooperative learning and made the working surfaces larger. The classroom became more manageable and Marta said that she circulated more freely, facilitating lessons and coaching students as required.

(Marta said she considered reducing the size of the "Magic Land City" landform, but opted to leave it unaltered, "because the larger the landform, the more realistic the simulation became to the students.")

"I noticed that my voice was now one of many in my class, not the only one," Marta said, adding that her students interacted with her and with each other because they felt that their opinions and suggestions were valued. Marta "felt less stress because pressure to adhere to a pacing guide was not my first concern, due to my students' eagerness to learn the required subject matter."

Validated by parents' and administrators' response to what she was doing, Marta saw that her "role as an educator was to promote critical thinking and curiosity for learning, rather than simply disseminating information."

2nd Grade

In 1972, veteran teacher Joanne Gram applied Design-Based Learning in her 2nd-grade classroom at Thomas Jefferson Elementary School in the Pasadena Unified School District. She wanted to teach her students about different forms of government to prepare them to govern the City they built and the classroom. Joanne had her students research four types of government—monarchy, anarchy, dictatorship, and democracy—by making a chart listing the basic characteristics of each. She told them they could apply what they learned to determine class activities for an hour a day for one week, including snack time.

"I explained that they were going to play a government game and that once it started, I would not interfere in any way," she said. "They would be totally in charge."

To start, the students agreed unanimously that they didn't want a leader at all, and chose anarchy so that they could do whatever they pleased. Soon, arguments developed over who could do what, and some students grew bored. They asked Joanne for something else to do.

"I refused," she said. "I told them I couldn't help, because if no one was in charge, that meant me, too."

The students swiftly responded by choosing a monarchy with a king and queen. At snack time, when fruit was served, the king and queen declared that because they were royal they should each have two pieces of fruit, and their subjects only one. After a few grumbles from the "subjects," the queen announced that anyone stepping out of line would have to write "I will obey" 15 times. Several children asked Joanne to stop the game, but when she again refused, one student,

Veronica, circulated a secret petition that she take over because the rulers were unfair. Ninety-five percent of the class signed, and the next day, when the game hour continued, Veronica was in control.

Veronica was generous and fair on her first day as dictator and all went smoothly. The following day, power went to her head and she became bossy. The students signed a second petition stating that they were tired of Veronica telling them what to do and didn't want a dictatorship anymore. On the fifth and last day of Joanne's government game, the students held an election for a Mayor and, surprisingly, former dictator Veronica was unanimously elected. This time, she gave no orders; instead, all of the students voted on what they determined to be important issues about their City and classroom.

"As I hoped," Joanne said, "this turned out to be a profound experience for the students in their comprehension of the meaning of government and democracy. It changed the classroom."

(That an experiment like this could happen today, with parent and administrative approval, is perhaps unlikely, but this was the 1970s when there was a great deal of experimentation in how the curriculum was delivered. The parents and administration were informed beforehand about the academic intention of Joanne's weeklong, one hour a day, government game, and about students' potential reactions to it.)

2nd Grade

Starting in 1999, Terry Ceja, a virtuoso teacher then in the Hacienda-La Puente Unified School District, took the rearrangement of her classroom to an imaginative extreme. After recess one afternoon, as her 2nd graders filed into the classroom, Terry dimmed the lights and asked the students to gather around the long table used for group work. She had covered it with a tablecloth and placed an ornate candelabra in the center, aglow with flame-shaped light bulbs. Instead of plates, there were books at each place setting. Asked to pick up the books,

Terry's awed students handled them with care, seeing them through new eyes: suddenly, books were special.

In Terry's classroom, this kind of innovative visual and spatial engagement was a daily occurrence. It was how she lured her underserved student population into a love of reading and learning. Rotating reading groups met with Terry in a corner of the room furnished with a small sofa, an armchair, and a coffee table. When she became a Design-Based Learning teacher, the "Creature Land" City her students were building was positioned nearby on a table with a map of its real-world location hanging above it. The books Terry selected for her Guided Lessons in each of her reading groups related in some way to her question of the day about "Creature Land." Bringing the groups together to discuss what they had read and how it connected to "Creature Land," Terry encouraged her students to get up and look at what they were building, read the map, and refer to their books.

The interdisciplinary questions they discussed led to other Guided Lessons. The students learned to calculate distances from one part of "Creature Land" to another as a Math lesson. They learned about Civics and Government by pretending to be City Council Members. They decided on height limits for their "Creature Land" buildings and voted on modes of movement throughout the City.

Armed with pencil and paper in their study groups, the 2nd graders learned to take notes about what was decided so that they could report to the whole class at the next "Creature Land" town meeting. Terry held these meetings for five minutes the first thing in the morning to go over the daily agenda, and for five minutes at the end of the day to summarize daily events.

This form of academic play reaped significant benefits for Terry's students. In a school with exceptionally low attendance and test scores, Terry created a welcoming classroom environment and used her storytelling ability to weave compelling reasons for learning. Her class had the highest attendance rate in the whole school. Terry's students came to school even when they were sick and had to be sent home. Behavior problems were rarities and her students' academic test scores soared.

3rd Grade

Dolores Patton and Leslie Barclay, teachers who applied my method of Design-Based Learning at the LA Open Magnet Elementary School for the Apple Computer Vivarium Project (see Chapter 5), had a double classroom consisting of 70 3rd-grade students. Their classroom, called the Yellow Cluster, had little room for storage and was so crowded with stuff that students' backpacks and lunches were often switched or lost. There was always some crisis about where to find what, and too much time during the school day was spent just trying to locate what was needed for learning.

Dolores and Leslie decided to involve the students in designing some solutions. They guided the students to take an inventory of the different kinds of items to be stored and to develop a checkout system for keeping things in order. They agreed with the students that boxes of old books and files that hadn't been looked at for over 10 years should be removed, and that two of the newly emptied closets would be devoted to backpacks. The Backpack Commissioner (who was also the Commissioner of Health for the student-built City) oversaw the putting away and retrieving of them. Voila! Once the classroom was reconfigured, living in the classroom space was less chaotic. The Yellow Cluster students learned big lessons about categorization, the function of things, who gets to decide what goes where, and how supplies are managed.

More than 30 years later, new teachers in the Yellow Cluster classroom continue practicing the Design-Based Learning methodology.

High School (Special English Language Development)

Araceli Garcia, working with two other teachers at Workman High School in the Hacienda-La Puente Unified School District, taught English Language Development through Design-Based Learning. The 90-minute English classes took place once a week over a school year. Araceli's 30 9th- to 12th-grade students came from all over, including the Philippines, Costa Rica, and Mexico. Typically, some students had been in the country for only a few months and required constant translation; others had differing levels of English fluency.

"Having a student-driven classroom that integrates hands-on learning," Araceli said, "allows students' affective filter to decrease, leading to less stress and greater ease in speaking English." (The term "affective filter" describes possible psychological barriers to learning a second language.)

Following the current research thinking about language acquisition, Araceli had her students learn to speak English in pairs so they could speak "Language ONE" (their native language) and learn "Language TWO" (English).

To further promote English Language fluency, Araceli gave her students the Design Challenge of building Never-Before-Seen Shelters for their individual Creature/Avatars. She put her students in teams to build eight small Starter Cities of the Future and had them decide where their Shelters belonged and why. Each City had a team leader (the Mayor), task manager (the Secretary), a Building Supply Manager, and a Treasurer. Araceli said, "I clung to my Criteria List as a tool for presenting English vocabulary—nouns and adjectives—that I required they use to describe the Shelters and the City that they were building."

At first, when she told her students that they would have to individually present their designs orally in English and asked for volunteers, they grumbled, Araceli said. "But once the presentations began, all of the students willingly spoke English to describe everything they built." After the initial presentations, Araceli had the students put all eight of their small Cities together to make a big one, prompting spirited discussions in English about what City should go where and why.

The data that Araceli collected in these classes from small samples of students on multiple tests, including a reading comprehension exam, confirmed that all these students made significant academic improvements.

Araceli said that she plans to build a Professional Learning Community (PLC) of teachers at Workman High School who apply the Design-Based Learning methodology to their subject field, and to present this successful practice to expand the training throughout her district and beyond.

MAKING CURRICULUM PHYSICAL

Delivering a Long-Range, Integrated, Design-Based Learning Curriculum

LONG-RANGE PLANNING BOARDS IN DEPTH

Long-Range Planning Boards matter. The time it takes to fabricate them is worth it, because this highly visual and tactile process invariably leads teachers to an invaluable "aha" recognition that developing a monthly integrated curriculum with Design-Based Learning is doable: "Look, I can teach spelling here," "I can have students calculate measurements here," or "I can connect a Design Challenge about Movement to a study of the human circulatory system here."

Long-Range Planning Boards are large (approximately 30 × 20 inches each) to dramatize that a sequence of Design Challenges with cross-subject Guided Lessons, represents an integrated curriculum. They are meant to be visible to everyone, a colorful and tactile roadmap of what has been accomplished and what is coming next, piquing the curiosity of students, from kindergartners to high schoolers. Students can see where their teacher's **BIG TOPIC** Design Challenges and related Guided Lessons (**small topics**) will take them as the semester or school year progresses, and where they are in the "story" that the teacher expands as students identify dilemmas in their Starter City and go on to solve through a sequence of Design Challenges with Guided Lessons. These portable Boards can be presented to parents and other teachers, and can be carried to district and school meetings, staff development trainings, and conferences. If teachers change grade levels or if the curriculum changes, the Boards are easily reconfigured.

("When I was a teacher in the Los Angeles Unified School District," said Jessica Heim, UCLA's Center X Director of the Design-Based Learning Project, "I lost my 1st-grade spot. I got placed in the 5th grade, which I never would have chosen. I was panicked over what to teach, but when I looked at the Long-Range Planning Boards that I had made for the 1st grade, I discovered that all I had to do was to change my Guided Lessons to meet the 5th-grade standards and reorder my Design Challenges. My principal was impressed and my students thrived.")

When I teach teachers how to make Long-Range Planning Boards, I do it the way I teach everything else: backwards. I have them focus on the visual aspects of the Long-Range Planning Boards and spend what may seem to be an inordinate amount of time teaching about how to make an easily readable display of color-coded, standards-based subject matter. The discussion of color and the aesthetics of the Boards is my way of engaging teachers in making a visual display that shows all of the inter-curricular connections that each Design Challenge generates. (Many teachers I work with have not had to consider the readability of materials or the power of color as a tool to organize, display, and present information.)

Before teachers begin making their first Board, they identify a **BIG TOPIC** that they are required to teach at their grade level or in their subject area. They select sheets of cardstock in the colors they have chosen to represent different aspects of their curriculum. They choose one color to represent all of their **BIG TOPIC** Design Challenges. They select different colors to represent each subject area and its required Guided Lessons and the specific standard to be taught. They choose another color to represent both governance and management of the student-built City and the classroom.

Elementary school teachers display all their subjects on their Boards; middle and high school teachers display a concentration of core curriculum related to the subject being taught.

I ask teachers to consider the size and clarity of the font they choose to print on their selected colors. Will their Long-Range Planning Boards be readable to students, parents, and others? They cut each colored sheet, printed with their Guided Lessons in separate subject areas, into 4- × 4-inch cards. They make a color-coded, multichanneled, detachable legend on a 30-inch strip of poster board that can be easily moved monthly from Board to Board and is the template for 5 to 10 Boards (depending on the length of each teacher's school term). They insert each of their cards into plastic pockets attached to the appropriate color-coded channel on their Boards.

Now, I get to the meat of my Backwards Thinking™ process: teachers refine and personalize their Long-Range Planning Boards. They add required Guided Lessons that best relate to each Design Challenge by using words that adhere to the higher-level thinking skills as described in Bloom's *Taxonomy*. For example, "compare" and "contrast" versus such lower-level words as "recall" or "name." Teachers refer to the State Curriculum Framework for their grade level to find the mandated higher-level thinking words that describe their Guided Lessons. (Teachers often express relief that the State Curriculum Framework, the source of their district requirements, brings clarity to what they are expected to teach.) On a computer, they make a new grid of squares. In each square, they write out their additional Guided Lessons above the name, number, and short description of the corresponding standard written in a smaller font. For each month's Design Challenge, teachers print out their grid of Guided Lessons and standards on the cardstock that matches the color they've chosen for each subject area, according to their moveable legend.

Once refined and organized, Long-Range Planning Boards do not have to be remade. They can be shuffled and reconfigured as subject matter changes, and parts can be replaced when new grade levels are assigned.

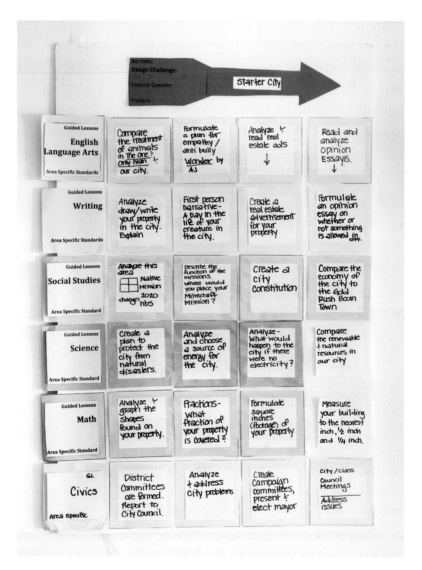

Georgia Singleton's Long-Range Planning Board for her 4th graders' Starter City with plastic pockets displaying multi-subject Guided Lessons on cards that can be easily arranged and rearranged.

At the elementary level, each of the 10 sections of a teacher's Long-Range Planning Boards would have six channels of color representing high-level Guided Lessons and standards from six subject areas, printed on cardstock in a family of related, pale colors for readability. Each **BIG TOPIC** Design Challenge is named on brightly colored cardstock, so it is the first thing a viewer notices. Anyone looking at the Long-Range Planning Boards can see at a glance what Design Challenges and Guided Lessons students are working on.

By making Long-Range Planning Boards to display a sequential, integrated curriculum, teachers applying the Design-Based Learning methodology refine all aspects of their teaching practice, and become fluent in seeking out a wider array of curricular connections.

Examples of Long-Range Planning Boards

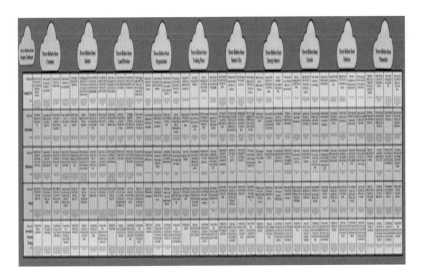

Color-coded channels on Long-Range Planning Boards displaying an entire school year, made by Lynn Fisher, 2nd-grade teacher, McKinley Elementary School, San Gabriel Unified School District.

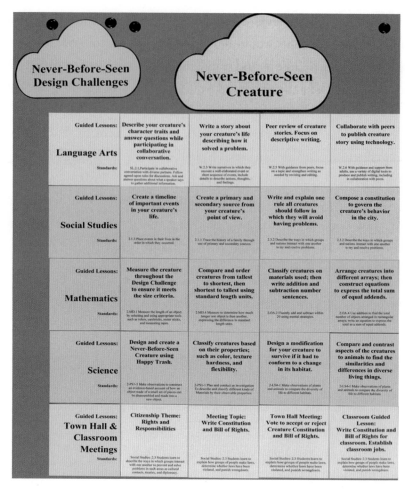

	Never-Before-Seen Design Challenges	Never-Before-Seen Creature		
Language Arts — Guided Lessons:	Describe your creature's character traits and answer questions while participating in collaborative conversation.	Write a story about your creature's life describing how it solved a problem.	Peer review of creature stories. Focus on descriptive writing.	Collaborate with peers to publish creature story using technology.
Standards:	SL.2.1 Participate in collaborative conversation with diverse partners. Follow agreed-upon rules for discussions. Ask and answer questions about what a speaker says to gather additional information.	W.2.3 Write narratives in which they recount a well-elaborated event or short sequence of events, include details to describe the actions, thoughts, and feelings.	W.2.5 With guidance from peers, focus on a topic and strengthen writing as needed by revising and editing.	W.2.6 With guidance and support from adults, use a variety of digital tools to produce and publish writing, including in collaboration with peers.
Social Studies — Guided Lessons:	Create a timeline of important events in your creature's life.	Create a primary and secondary source from your creature's point of view.	Write and explain one rule all creatures should follow in which they will avoid having problems.	Compose a constitution to govern the creature's behavior in the city.
Standards:	2.1.3 Place events in their lives in the order in which they occurred.	2.1.1 Trace the history of a family through use of primary and secondary sources.	2.3.2 Describe the ways in which groups and nations interact with one another to try and resolve problems.	2.3.2 Describe the ways in which groups and nations interact with one another to try and resolve problems.
Mathematics — Guided Lessons:	Measure the creature throughout the Design Challenge to ensure it meets the size criteria.	Compare and order creatures from tallest to shortest, then shortest to tallest using standard length units.	Classify creatures on materials used; then write addition and subtraction number sentences.	Arrange creatures into different arrays; then construct equations to express the total sum of equal addends.
Standards:	2.MD.1 Measure the length of an object by selecting and using appropriate tools such as rulers, yardsticks, meter sticks, and measuring tapes.	2.MD.4 Measure to determine how much longer one object is than another, expressing the difference in standard length units.	2.OA.2 Fluently add and subtract within 20 using mental strategies.	2.OA.4 Use addition to find the total number of objects arranged in rectangular arrays; write an equation to express the total as a sum of equal addends.
Science — Guided Lessons:	Design and create a Never-Before-Seen Creature using Happy Trash.	Classify creatures based on their properties; such as color, texture hardness, and flexibility.	Design a modification for your creature to survive if it had to conform to a change in its habitat.	Compare and contrast aspects of the creatures to animals to find the similarities and differences in diverse living things.
Standards:	2-PS1-3 Make observations to construct an evidence-based account of how an object made of a small set of pieces can be disassembled and made into a new object.	2-PS1-1 Plan and conduct an investigation to describe and classify different kinds of materials by their observable properties.	2-LS4-1 Make observations of plants and animals to compare the diversity of life in different habitats.	2-LS4-1 Make observations of plants and animals to compare the diversity of life in different habitats.
Town Hall & Classroom Meetings — Guided Lessons:	Citizenship Theme: Rights and Responsibilities	Meeting Topic: Write Constitution and Bill of Rights.	Town Hall Meeting: Vote to accept or reject Creature Constitution and Bill of Rights.	Classroom Guided Lesson: Write Constitution and Bill of Rights for classroom. Establish classroom jobs.
Standards:	Social Studies 2.3 Students learn to describe the ways in which groups interact with one another to prevent and solve problems in such areas as cultural contacts, treaties, and diplomacy.	Social Studies 2.3 Students learn to explain how groups of people make laws, determine whether laws have been violated, and punish wrongdoers.	Social Studies 2.3 Students learn to explain how groups of people make laws, determine whether laws have been violated, and punish wrongdoers.	Social Studies 2.3 Students learn to explain how groups of people make laws, determine whether laws have been violated, and punish wrongdoers.

A close-up of 2nd-grade teacher Lynn Fisher's Long-Range Planning Board showing her legend and one month of Guided Lessons.

Long-Range Planning Boards and History Wall combined, organized by Natalie Bezdjian, Kindergarten teacher, Rose & Alex Pilibos Armenian School, Hollywood, California.

Through the prominent display of her Long-Range Planning Boards, Annette Dellemonico taught her middle school ESL students the vocabulary of her planning for the school year and had them check off what they completed as a review of the relationship between the Design Challenges and Guided Lessons.

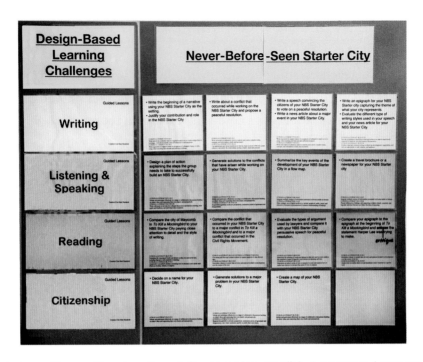

A Long-Range Planning Board for teaching English Language Learners developed by Stephanie Na, ELL teacher, Workman High School, Hacienda-La Puente Unified School District, showing a legend with main topics and one month of Guided Lessons.

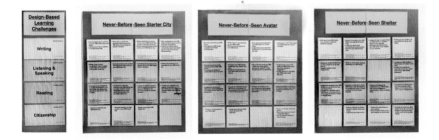

Stephanie Na's three-month plan with her legend and Guided Lessons.

THE EVOLUTION OF THE PLANNING PROCESS

Early on, teachers studying my methodology were having trouble developing their integrated, yearlong curriculum. The usual paper-pencil-computer process was confusing them and took too long. I was preaching the importance of the spatial domain in having students make sense of information, but I wasn't giving teachers that experience. After all, the spatial domain, where my methodology lives, is the most powerful way to teach and learn.

I struggled to find a tactile, time-efficient way to teach the making of Long-Range Planning Boards as a three-dimensional alternative to two-dimensional long-range planning. I remembered using a wooden orange crate as a container for developing a sequential, integrated curriculum during the last course I took at UCLA before achieving my degree and teaching credential. Unofficially called "The Seeds Box," this course was developed by Corinne Seeds, a John Dewey disciple, for whom the Seeds University Elementary School at UCLA was named, and it was taught by *her* disciple, Charlotte Crabtree. The requirement for the final exam, based on Dewey's philosophical pedagogy of learning by doing, was to develop a comprehensive course of study around such K–6 units as Community, Early California, the Pilgrims, the Westward Movement, the United Nations, or Japan. The point was to learn how major topics in the social sciences were the nuclei for hands-on activities and lessons to connect subject matter with basic skills across the curriculum.

The orange crates housed our step-by-step, yearlong, cross-curricular teaching sequences. Each step in a sequence specified the actual Reading, Math, Science, Language Arts, Music, and Art lessons related to a topic and described both the physical artifacts that students would build and their subsequent research and textbook studies. Adhering to the details required to make a "Seeds Box" taught me to study state and district requirements and to use textbooks and other resources to amplify subject matter. The end result was a course of study that made sense to me and readied me for teaching.

With the "Seeds Box" in mind, I devised an activity called "The Red Cups," using plastic, flat-bottomed red cups as containers and a three-dimensional representation of the red triangle on the Curriculum Integration Chart. Having teachers fill their Red Cups with written Guided Lessons related to each Design Challenge, I thought, would clarify their thinking about how to integrate their Design-Based Learning curriculum. I eventually replaced the Red Cups with 3D Red Triangles because the flat-bottomed Red Cups gave teachers the wrong visual cue.

The 3D Red Triangles speed up learning for teachers like crazy. The 3D Red Triangles, the Curriculum Integration Chart, and the Long-Range Planning Boards (see Chapter 4), facilitate the development of a comprehensive, sequential, integrated curriculum. Teachers become expertly familiar with the mandatory state standards, and as part of their long-range planning process, they identify ways to teach higher-level thinking skills as well as the speaking and writing skills required across subjects and grade levels.

ACTIVATING A YEARLONG, STORY-DRIVEN CURRICULUM

The following examples describe the application of long-range plans developed and activated by graduates of the Design-Based Learning master's degree program, which began in 1995 at Cal Poly Pomona, providing a sequential context for up to 10 Design Challenges, each followed by a series of related daily Guided Lessons.

The Newlandia Story (High School, Special Needs)

Don Huey was a seasoned teacher who taught U.S. History, World History, Government, and Life Science to underserved students with special needs at Ganesha High School in the Pomona Unified School District when he received the first Design-Based Learning master's degree. During his course work, Don complained bitterly about the requirement to have his students build a tabletop City. I told him that he could do anything he wanted to do as long as it was three-dimensional, and was based on a real location as the setting for a sequential story that evolved as students identified and solved problems. I didn't have a clue how to apply these constraints to all of the subjects Don taught, but I knew that building a City in the classroom worked.

Don developed his story sequence around what he called "Newlandia," which had four Colonies to simulate the development of the United States. He invented an island in a real-world location in the Pacific Ocean to impose geographic constraints and made a 3D landscape representing that location. Don even figured out where to put the model in his crowded classroom, by raising it on pulleys to the ceiling when it was not in use.

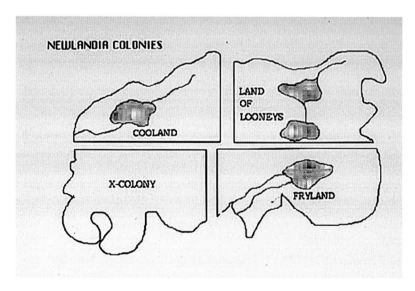

High school teacher Don Huey's map of Newlandia's four Colonies.

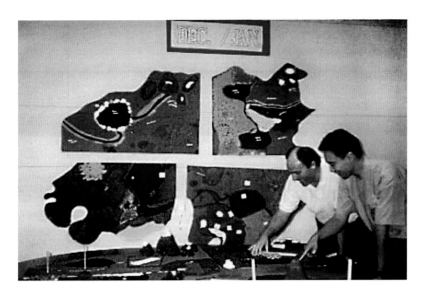

The tabletop land site for Newlandia, corresponding to the painted map on the wall.

Don's high school students, who had had little to no creative hands-on activity since early grade school, couldn't wait to "play" in Newlandia. His World History students role-played a scenario that they learned afterward in Guided Lessons that were based on events that occurred during World War I. Don specified varied biomes for his Science class. He put his Government class in charge of developing and communicating the rules and regulations governing Newlandia that were adhered to by all of his classes.

One mildly autistic student was so motivated by his experience in building creative solutions to Design Challenges that he entered a contest sponsored by the Toyota Corporation to design a futuristic car. The student insisted that he could do this because a carrier that he had designed for the movement system in Newlandia had been approved by all four classes. He submitted photos of his carrier along with his completion of all the paperwork required for the contest. With Don's guidance, the student met the deadline and although he didn't win, he was thrilled to receive a letter from Toyota praising his efforts.

In that first Design-Based Learning master's degree program, Don's cohort group was very small. Although he joined the others in asking lots of questions, he did not communicate his frustrations or concerns easily in class. At the end of each of our four-hour weekly meetings, I was always unnerved when Don would slam the classroom door as he left. I met with him, suggesting that because he seemed so upset, perhaps this was not the program for him. "No!" he responded. "Every week when I leave class, I'm so mad that I never learned this before, and that all the kids I taught during my 20 years in the classroom never benefited from this kind of teaching."

The Spanishtopia Story (Middle School, Spanish)

The story of Spanishtopia was developed by Martha Jimenez-Corsi over two years, teaching three different groups of students at three different locations: Wilson Middle School, Eliot Middle School, and Washington Middle School in the Pasadena Unified School District. Through a sequence of Design Challenges for their tabletop City called Spanishtopia, students learned and used Spanish vocabulary, verb conjugation, and sentence structure to identify and describe the artifacts they built and revised and to govern their City.

When Martha's students identified that the creations they built for their Starter City—their first version of Spanishtopia—were indistinguishable from one another, they decided to rebuild Spanishtopia in an organized manner. They designed a Never-Before-Seen Way to Know Your Surroundings. In Guided Lessons, they learned the value of interpreting city signs, especially when visiting foreign countries. Learning the names of common city signs in Spanish, they analyzed ways that information is displayed in a city.

Martha's sequence of Design Challenges continued with students creating signage for Spanishtopia. They built Never-Before-Seen Inhabitants (Avatars) for their City and learned the Spanish names of body parts, titles of respect, and vocabulary to describe physical and personality traits. They practiced speaking Spanish by introducing their Inhabitants to others. When Martha suggested that their Inhabitants were too much alike, the students designed Never-Before-Seen Personal Adornment and learned the Spanish vocabulary related to clothing, accessories, and how weather conditions affect clothing choices. Through class discussion, students analyzed how clothing and personal adornment are part of self-identity, cultural values, and geographic location.

The students met their Inhabitants' everyday needs by designing Never-Before-Seen Places to Exchange Goods and learning the names of common businesses and merchandise in Spanish. To enable their Inhabitants to get around in Spanishtopia, they designed a Never-Before-Seen Way to Move and had Guided Lessons on how to request transportation services and schedules in Spanish. They filled empty spaces in their small City with Never-Before-Seen Ways to Entertain, learning to use basic vocabulary related to leisure activities, and comparing how those activities were the same or different in other cultures.

At the end of Martha's comprehensive sequence of Design Challenges, a community had been established. Students designed a Never-Before-Seen Course Keepsake as a memory holder to review and evaluate what they had learned.

"Spanishtopia was a revelation," Martha said. "It not only improved my teaching practices, but it so thoroughly captured the interest of my students, that it was clear that Spanish class became truly relevant to them."

The Atomic City Story (High School Chemistry)

Temy Taylor taught Chemistry at Ganesha High School. Her students built a tabletop City to learn about molecules and atoms. Temy activated her Atomic City story by having students build and revise their City as a molecular world.

All it took to get students started was to have them draw a single dot on a piece of paper to represent an atom. The students observed that no two dots looked alike. Temy had them close their eyes and imagine being the same size as their Dots. They dressed up as Dots (in sandwich boards made of butcher paper) to make the characteristics of their Dots visible to everyone. They discussed how their Dots looked and felt and what it might be like to go inside them. The students then built paper replicas of their Dots, making them small enough to move around in Atomic City. Over the months, students revised their City, responding to a progression of more complex Design Challenges followed by related Guided Lessons about the Periodic Table, bonding, compounds, nuclear chemistry, energy, matter, intra-molecular forces, art, and history.

For one Design Challenge, Temy had her students group their Dots into families in Atomic City. Preparing students for Guided Lessons on how atoms bond, Temy's Criteria List included the requirement that the Dots had to share at least one similarity. (In chemistry, atoms with similar characteristics are called a family or group and are represented by each column of the Periodic Table.) Once the students' families of Dots congregated in Atomic City, like many atoms bonding together, they became bigger compounds called macromolecules.

The Atomic City story continued as students' Dots came under attack when Temy pretended to be an unknown force randomly redistributing the Dots around the City. As the students designed ways to scatter their Dots to escape the attack, they learned about nuclear fusion and energy of reactions. After the attack, the new groups of Dots rebuilt Atomic City in their new locations. Temy used the new groupings to teach Guided Lessons about different types of compounds, and based on how the Dots arranged themselves in their rebuilt City, students learned about the forces that make up solids and liquids.

Through other Design Challenges with Guided Lessons related to the Dots in Atomic City, students learned about chemical equations, balancing equations, chemical equilibrium, and how chemistry is used for art in making pigments, dyes, and acid-base reactions. As the year ended, the students designed a Never-Before-Seen Way to Celebrate the Atomic City story and their achievements.

The Anomop City Story (High School, Language Arts)

Janet Perez had been in the business world for years before becoming a teacher. As a new high school English teacher in a difficult, underserved setting in the Pomona Unified School District, she came into the Design-Based Learning master's program to hone her skills. Even with her limited classroom experience, Janet was convinced that it was not enough for students to read a book about the Holocaust unless they could understand the value that society places on human life. She wanted them to not only become better readers, but to learn to be more empathic humans.

Janet had her students build a tabletop City and structured a sequential curriculum—her Anomop (Pomona spelled backwards) City Story—around a logical sequence of Design Challenges as they developed the City over the course of the school year. Janet's sequence of Design Challenges began with a Never-Before-Seen Place to Learn (to get to know their classroom), Never-Before-Seen-Avatars to live in their City, and Never-Before-Seen Shelters for students' Avatars. Her students' ability to perform on standardized tests greatly improved, Janet observed, because they developed higher-level thinking skills. The hands-on Design Challenges targeted all students, including those with diverse learning styles. Janet described the willingness of her English Language Learners (ELLs) to practice speaking skills, resulting in their advanced reading and vocabulary development. According to Janet, over the course of the school year, her students became more motivated to participate in Design Challenges and grasped that learning can be derived from failure as well as success.

By placing herself outside of her comfort zone and exploring new ways to innovate in her classroom, Janet matured as an educator and was energized by her students' academic and creative growth.

The Special Kids City Story (Elementary School, Special Needs)

The yearlong Special Kids City Story was developed by Deborah Kostich, a teacher for students with moderate to severe disabilities in an elementary school in the Pasadena Unified School District. Her goal was to promote students' self-expression and socialization, develop their communication skills, expand their vocabulary, exercise their fine motor skills, and have them learn to apply subject matter information to the building of a tabletop City in the classroom.

Deborah engaged her students in 10 simple hands-on Design Challenges that told a rudimentary story about a City, the Special Kids who lived there, how they got around, and where they went. The Design Challenges were derived from all required subjects to provide an integrated, standards-based curriculum. Deborah's Special Kids Story encompassed her goals for each of her students and enabled her to assess their progress, check items completed on a daily basis, and modify Guided Lessons according to each student's weaknesses and needs.

Deborah's Long-Range Planning Boards created a flow for her entire Special Kids curriculum and gave her a visual tool that she showed to her students, their parents, and her administrators so that everyone knew what she was teaching—and she did, too.

Deborah's students made progress in meeting the Individualized Education Program (IEP) goals and objectives. They constructed their versions of Never-Before-Seen, three-dimensional artifacts for each Design Challenge as Deborah taught them to cut, glue, stack, and connect parts and related everything they did to subject matter. Her students' fine motor and exploration skills improved and as they described the artifacts they created, her students demonstrated that they could learn to think critically.

In her master's project, Deborah said that her way of teaching changed dramatically. Before applying the Design-Based Learning methodology, she had emphasized single objectives and integrated a minimal amount of physical projects in her planning. She had focused her lesson plans on teaching the objectives and observed that she had underestimated the importance of allowing time for her students to do creative, hands-on activities.

The Math City Story (Middle School Math)

Sharon Soto, a 6th-grade Math teacher in the Walnut Valley Unified School District (where the District built a middle school building dedicated to Design-Based Learning), said she had been a very traditional teacher and that, at first, Design-Based Learning was a stretch for her. The purpose of Sharon's integrated, standards-based, Math City curriculum was to promote higher-level thinking, creative problem solving, reasoning, and proficiency in Math, and to teach students to use and reuse what they learned in a variety of computational settings. To achieve her goals, Sharon taught her students to work collaboratively as they built a tabletop Math City of the Future in the classroom.

Sharon applied the Design-Based Learning methodology through a progression of Design Challenges in three of her courses: Math 6 (regular Math students, including limited English speakers, special education students, and gifted students), Basic Math (students, including some with special needs and non-English speakers, identified as struggling in Math by their 5th-grade teachers), and Advanced Math (students identified as advanced in Math by their 5th-grade teachers, including special education and gifted students). At first, Sharon was concerned about taking time away from teaching Math by having her students build a City. She felt that dealing with the logistics—acquiring building materials, dispersing the materials during the building process, and finding space to store or display the artifacts made for Design Challenges—would eat up too much of her preparation time for Math lessons.

Sharon noted that what kept her going was that even students who learned at a different pace from her Advanced Math students, looked forward to building and doing group work as they followed the Math City Story she gave them for context. Sharon taught these students to analyze their progress in learning mathematical concepts by using the Criteria List. They did not excel in the pencil and paper work or doing computations, but by referring to the Criteria List, they identified and solved mathematical problems during the building process that even some of her "good Math test takers" could not solve. Sharon found that when students were successful in one area, they put much more effort into their weaker areas.

Sharon observed that by devoting 15 to 45 minutes of her 50-minute class once a week to Design Challenges, she was able to engage her students in Guided Lessons and easily taught them about measurement, area, and geometry. Energized by her students' new enthusiasm for Math, Sharon comfortably justified the time spent building Math City, and developed an array of Guided Lessons connected to other related Math standards.

The Microdena Story (International Baccalaureate School, 3rd Grade)

After Leakana Nhem received her master's degree in Design-Based Learning, she deepened her focus on the methodology in an Education Leadership Doctoral program at Cal Poly Pomona.

Leakana's Microdena Story for her 3rd-grade students at Willard International Baccalaureate and Technology Magnet Elementary School in the Pasadena Unified School District took the form of a three-dimensional, student-built, small Community, reflecting the school's goal to promote citizenship and responsibility.

She developed her Microdena curriculum by identifying problems in the Community they built and linking one problem to another in a natural way. She taught her students to make connections between what happened in the Microdena Story and what happened in their larger community and in the world.

Leakana Nehm's students locating their Microdena land parcels on a map they made of their real community.

Prior to applying the Design-Based Learning methodology, Leakana said that she struggled to cope with disjointed curricula, with unrealistic pacing guides, teacher manuals, and student workbooks. Her Microdena Story was a yearlong plan for distributing learning among several subject areas. Her sequence of Never-Before-Seen Plant, Creature, and Structure Design Challenges emphasized how every natural and artificial form has a corresponding function. She connected Science, Math, Language Arts, Social Studies, and Art with each of her Design Challenges. Leakana's Long-Range Planning

Boards incorporated subject areas that she said due to time constraints she had previously often left out of the school day.

As an outline for her Long-Range Planning Boards, Leakana Nehm charted 10 Essential Questions, Design Problems, and corresponding Never-Before-Seen (NBS) Design Challenges that defined her Microdena Story for the school year:

Essential Question	Design Problem	NBS Design Challenge
How do humans learn about each other?	We need to get to know one another and the Design-Based Learning process.	1. NBS Introduction
How do symbolic representations portray and explain the self to others?	We need to get to know ourselves before we can empathize with and make friends with others.	2. NBS Body Object
How does a growing population shelter itself and have its needs met?	We need places for everyone to live, work, and play.	3. NBS Starter Community
How does the structure of living things affect human survival?	We need sources for food, water, and oxygen to survive.	4. NBS Plant
How do the life cycle and changes in habitat con-tribute to survival?	We need a food chain and an oxygen-carbon exchange cycle so our Creatures can live.	5. NBS Creature, Life Cycle

Essential Question	Design Problem	NBS Design Challenge
How do humans use available resources to protect themselves from dangers?	Our Creatures need protection in their community from the weather, natural disasters, and aggressors.	6. NBS Structure
How do humans decide what and how to move?	Our Creatures need to get from one place to another to exchange goods, obtain services, and for work and play.	7. NBS Way to Move
How does communication benefit humans?	Our Creatures do not have a means to communicate information and needs. Accidents happen because of this deficiency.	8. NBS Way to Communicate
How do humans capture and conserve energy?	Movement and communication systems in our community need constant power. We need to find new energy sources and save energy to meet Microdena's demands.	9. NBS Ways to Find and Conserve Energy
How do humans remember and preserve their past?	A review of the year: now that Microdena has progressed and advanced technologically, structurally, and socially, we need to preserve its story for future generations.	10. NBS Way to Be Remembered Forever

CHAPTER 19

THE HISTORY WALL

An Evolving Review of Classroom Learning

One 2nd-grade teacher, a student in the Design-Based Learning Certificate Program at Cal Poly Pomona, had offered her portable classroom as a weekly meeting place for her cohort group of K–12 teachers. One evening's topic was the History Wall. I was introducing the teachers in the program to ways to use classroom walls to engage students in an ongoing review of their yearlong participation in Design-Based Learning by displaying a record of their Design Challenges and academic experiences that would evolve monthly.

The History Wall does for teachers what the City does for students: it displays the parts that make up a contextual whole.

The bulletin boards in this teacher's portable classroom were tightly bordered with scalloped paper, the kind sold by the yard for teachers to use to decorate their classrooms. She invited a discussion about ways her classroom walls could capture her students' learning experiences as they built their tabletop City, governed it and the classroom, and learned the grade-level curriculum through Guided Lessons.

To begin the discussion, I asked everyone for out-of-the-box thinking and had them look around the classroom for examples of traditional in-the-box thinking as well. They all noticed the meticulously framed bulletin boards, but didn't see the tiny stick figure pinned below one scalloped border until one of the teachers pointed it out. She laughed, saying that the figure was out-of-the-box and looked as if it were about to enter the constricted space of the bulletin board. A lively exchange took place about why the figure was outside the frame, why it was so small, and what message was being sent to students.

The teacher's response was that she had no idea why she put it there, but once it was pointed out, she and the other teachers reflected on the secondary messages being communicated. They were surprised by how many they came up with: kids may feel disconnected from their work, kids are too small to be part of the display, a stick figure is not stable or very important, the figure was outside the box because there was not enough room for kids, tiny people can go outside the box, but not real people.

As a rule, formal teacher training describes the walls of the classroom as a place to "advertise" learning with slogans and posters, display student work, or to remind students of their times tables, the alphabet, Periodic Table, etc. Sometimes, the display is done just to make the room look "pretty."

In my Design-Based Learning methodology, *everything* in the classroom, from the arrangement of furniture to what is on the walls, can serve as a tool for promoting problem seeking and problem solving. Developing a History Wall gives teachers deliberate reasons for what is displayed, reducing the time-consuming, random use of classroom walls. The cumulative process of making a History Wall takes the pressure off the teacher, as the classroom walls are always ready for review and presentation by students to administrators, parents on Back-to-School-Night, and to any other visitors.

A History Wall display developed by a teacher with student input enables students to see that their life in the classroom *is* history. A timeline on the walls as an ongoing review of the progression of their academic achievements makes students' classroom life visible. It teaches students that just as history books are written by those who decide what historic events to include and how much space is devoted to those events—they can be decision-makers, too.

My vision for the History Wall display of a Design-Based Learning, integrated curriculum in the classroom crystallized in 1971 when renowned designers Ray and Charles Eames gave me space in their office for the making of a film about my methodology. At that time, the Eameses were preparing an exhibition about Benjamin Franklin, Thomas Jefferson, and the founding of America. Commissioned by the U.S. government for the Bicentennial, their exhibit was to travel worldwide. It included artifacts on a timeline with horizontal, color-coded channels that represented different categories and topics related to the lives of these two Founding Fathers. This floor-to-ceiling exhibit featured the major events and artifacts associated with the founding of our country, the significant people of the time, and the related events that occurred concurrently all over the world.

Inspired by the Eames exhibition, the classroom History Wall evolved as I worked with teachers to change what is ordinarily seen on classroom walls by determining a comprehensive way to display a timeline of students' classroom life and learning. No two History Walls are the same. Teachers decide the criteria for having work placed on the History Wall. They decide how the History Wall is organized to show time, different topics and categories, how revisions are shown, when, why, and how much student work goes up on the History Wall, and when it is to be changed.

Not every teacher has the time to involve students in deciding the how and why of displaying a timeline of their experiences in the classroom, but explaining to students the reasons for the display promotes a student-centered classroom. This engagement in decision-making may not work for very young students. Teachers with rotating single subject classes can develop a portable History Wall to use as a review with students.

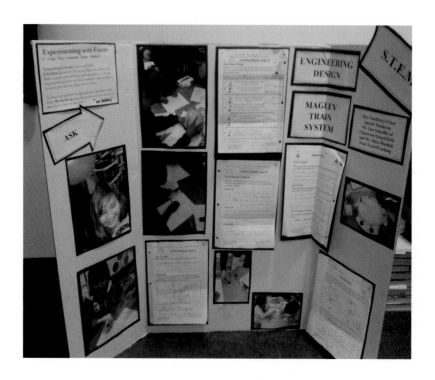

The portable History Wall (above) shows Guided Lessons resulting from one Design Challenge in Janice Sandberg's 3rd-grade mul-
tiple-subject class at Washington Accelerated Elementary School in
Pasadena, CA. To make her revolving, portable History Wall, Janice, a
graduate of the Design-Based Learning master's degree program at Cal
Poly, Pomona, developed the Criteria List below.

DON'T WANTS	NEEDS
Commercial Displays	Never-Before-Seen History Wall
Only Two-Dimensional Displays	Three-dimensional artifacts of student work in rotation
Random Order	Sequence showing evolution of Design Challenges
Only High Achievers Work	Criteria Lists for each Design Challenge

DON'T WANTS	NEEDS
	Samples of students' initial and revised versions of 3D artifacts for each Design Challenge
	Samples of Guided Lessons with color-coded subjects in separate channels
	Sample booklets that contain every student's written work about each Design Challenge
	Achievements and Assessments

THE HISTORY WALL IN THE CLASSROOM

Examples from the Design-Based Learning Master's Degree Program at Cal Poly, Pomona

2nd Grade

Marta Rosales, a 2nd-grade teacher at James Madison Elementary School in the Pasadena Unified School District, developed a collective History Wall as her students built their Magic Land City. She divided her classroom walls into 11 sequential sections representing the Magic Land Story as a timeline showing each Design Challenge and specific, standards-driven Guided Lessons.

"My History Wall and Long-Range Planning Boards served as a giant, visual pacing guide. To build suspense and anticipation, I revealed the Design Challenge titles named on my Long-Range Planning Boards to my students one at a time, and they enjoyed predicting what would happen next. The History Wall became a record-keeping document reflecting their progress through activities and expressions of critical thinking. Teaching my students to check the History Wall regularly gave them a constant review of their learning. For me, the History Wall became a tool for holding myself accountable, because it visually displayed the essence of what I was teaching every day.

"Parents' support of Magic Land grew during the year. At Open House, parents noted in particular that I had taught their children to articulate, rationalize, and explain their Design Challenges and Guided Lessons displayed on the History Wall. They were impressed by the level of academic vocabulary that their children had acquired and used on a daily basis during the year.

The History Wall informed parents, administrators, students—and me—about what the methodology of Design-Based Learning achieved in my classroom. It assured me that I was teaching the required curriculum in-depth and I felt comfortable about Backwards Thinking™."

High School (Chemistry)

"My History Wall took up most of the available wall space in the classroom," wrote Ganesha High School Chemistry teacher Temy Taylor, whose 10th–12th graders spent a semester building their Atomic City to learn chemistry. "At first, I felt that developing a History Wall display would take up more of my time than it was worth, until I saw what a significant impact it had on my students. The History Wall not only provided a review of the students' work throughout the school year, it was also a visual celebration. They retold their Atomic City story to each other and pointed with pride to their work on display. The History Wall became a powerful record of student progress in the classroom throughout the school year, showcasing where they had started and the steps they took along the way as they learned the Chemistry curriculum."

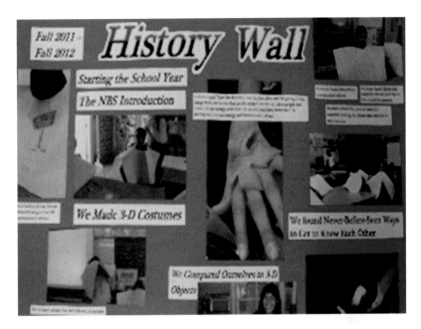

A poster made by Annette Dellemonico's ESL students showing the artifacts they built with captions identifying the progression of all Design Challenges.

Middle School (English as a Second Language [ESL])

Annette M. Dellemonico taught ESL at the Intermediate-Advanced (ESL 3) and Advanced (ESL 4) levels at Sepulveda Middle School in the Los Angeles Unified School District. "Each time a class completed a Design Challenge as they built their Paradise Hills City, and finished their Guided Lessons that connected the Design Challenge to their standards–based curriculum," she wrote, "my students put together a poster. By the end of the school year, there were 11 posters that illustrated each of my 11 Design Challenges with pictures of students working, pictures of their projects, narratives, work samples, and captions. Together, these 11 posters became my History Wall. As I developed the History Wall, the purpose of recording history became understandable to my students because they had a personal experience with documenting their own history. I taught them that history is written to remember experiences and to share knowledge and discoveries for those who come after us."

Middle School (Integrated Mathematics)

Robin Talbot, a teacher of Integrated Mathematics at Warner Middle School in the Westminster Unified School District, described the History Wall as "a visual reminder of the work done following each Design Challenge for my students' Biome City. During my first year of applying the Design-Based Learning methodology, I didn't start the History Wall until late in the year when I gave my students a Never-Before-Seen Festival Design Challenge. Not having visual reminders earlier in the year made a review of what was done previously somewhat difficult. My students were very clear about what they did in each Design Challenge, but they were less clear about the Guided Lessons connected to the Design Challenge.

"To maintain a stronger connection between the Design Challenges and the Guided Lessons in the second school year, I planned a History Wall and started it with the first Design Challenge. The Biome City class was just one of four classes that I taught. The amount of wall space devoted to a yearlong display of students' work in that class was minimal, so for my History Wall, I used the cabinets in the back of the classroom. With each new Design Challenge, I posted student work from the Guided Lessons along with their statements of the Math content. They read the History Wall as a reminder of the standards I taught and the work they did learning those standards. Having a History Wall in my classroom gave me insight about what to include or revise for the following school year—kind of a pre-plan for the next year."

10th Grade (English Language Arts)

10th-grade English Language Arts teacher Janet Perez at Ganesha High School in the Pomona Unified School District, wrote: "My

History Wall gave all of my students, not just 'the best,' a look back at the progress of their work over the course of the whole school year." Janet's History Wall covered an entire classroom wall. It was seen and discussed by the students, parents, and administrators to recall and examine student achievements. The History Wall was both descriptive and visual, documenting students' learning through photographs and thinking maps. Janet displayed student work from each of her 10 Design Challenges, by having students vote on the 5 to 10 most descriptive pieces of their work from each Design Challenge, then photographing their choices and putting them on the History Wall.

3rd Grade (English Language Learners [ELL] and Gifted and Talented Education [GATE])

"My History Wall was a visible timeline of what took place when students created their Island Adventure City," wrote Safini Lin Convey, a 3rd-grade ELL and GATE teacher at Mt. Washington Elementary School in the Los Angeles Unified School District.

"Each Design Challenge was successively posted and recorded with student work, revealing both their learning process and final products: photographs of students working on three-dimensional solutions, Guided Lessons and samples of their writing, geographical maps, graphs, science models, Math worksheets, and thinking maps. I taught both my ELL and my GATE students how to describe what was on the History Wall and how to prepare a tour for visitors.

"The day the principal came to visit, I had three students give her a tour of the History Wall. I didn't know what to expect of my 3rd graders, but they were so into it and she was so interested, that the tour went on for 30 minutes. Afterward, the principal commented: 'Each Design Challenge asked students to use their imagination while using critical-thinking skills to stay within certain assigned parameters. The students clearly understood their Design Challenge tasks as they worked within their own ability level to create Never-Before-Seen artifacts. The students were able to retain information as they enthusiastically explained their Design Challenges in depth. The level of critical thinking in these Never-Before-Seen creations is clear with the consistent use of Criteria Lists so that students self-monitor their work. They showed evidence of metacognition as they explained their learning in terms of both processes and products.' "

Middle School (Spanish Language)

"Creating a History Wall that displayed what I taught was new for me, as I usually had student work displayed randomly all over the classroom," said middle school Spanish teacher Martha Jimenez-Corsi. "I developed Spanishtopia City to sustain my students' interest in learning Spanish and to teach critical thinking skills. After each Design Challenge and its Guided Lessons, I had students select the assignments and the sequence they wanted to display on the History Wall. I noticed that they analyzed their work carefully before deciding what to display. My students even began bringing visitors into the classroom to see the History Wall and show off what they had done.

"Spanishtopia was well-received in all three middle schools where I taught. When administrators conducted random visits and observed the building and revision of the students' Spanishtopia Cities and the History Wall displays in each of my classrooms, my students acted as tour guides. They explained how the History Wall with my Long-Range Planning Boards displayed the curricular sequence for the course and the administrators easily saw the evidence that my Design Challenges and Guided Lessons were indeed teaching students the required Spanish curriculum."

2nd Grade

Joseph Lechner, a 2nd-grade teacher at Orangewood Elementary School in the West Covina Unified School District, graduated from the master's program in 2017.

"My History Wall was a living structure that celebrated my students' learning as they built their small Cloud City of the Future. It was ever-changing, displaying their artifacts, writing, and other representations of their learning, as I facilitated discussions with my students about what to add or remove. For example, my 2015–2016 students chose to display the Never-Before-Seen Creatures' Driver's Licenses that they made during a Guided Lesson after they built Never-Before-Seen Carriers and Pathways. My 2016–2017 students chose to display the land deeds that they wrote after building a Never-Before-Seen Way to Divide Land.

"The sampling of permanent and temporary items on display showed the progression of my Design-Based Learning curriculum throughout the school year. Having students choose what to display on the History Wall was another way to promote a student-centered classroom. It increased student engagement, participation, and ownership.

"My Criteria Lists, which I taught my students to refer to for self-assessment, were a permanent component of my History Wall. They were a visual set of directions for each of my Design Challenges. Other permanent components of my History Wall included the city map that represented the residential area around the school and the students' vision for Cloud City, a display shelf where completed artifacts were showcased (until they were approved by the Cloud City government to become part of the landsite), and a Committee Job Board, posting students' assigned committees and job responsibilities in the classroom and in Cloud City.

"When students took their individual Cloud City land parcels to their desks to make design changes, I repeatedly had them refer to the city map on the wall with its simple number grid to reassemble their City. I required that they apply Math skills to find the location of their land parcels so they could accurately put the City back together. I placed the display shelf at an appropriate height for students to have convenient access to their artifacts as I taught Guided Lessons and as they subsequently revised what they built for each Design Challenge. I used the Committee Job Board (a white board) as a changing list of students' jobs to teach about division of labor in a democratic society. I had students write their own job descriptions and I called regular, time-limited 'town meetings' to remind them of what their jobs entailed and to discuss how any problems that arose might be handled. I taught the students to refer to the Committee Job Board to find the appropriate person to talk to when there was a problem. For example, when some students weren't clearing their desks at the end of the day, their peers consulted the Building Inspector/Desk Monitor, who posted a reminder on the bulletin board.

"A variety of Cloud City-related student writing included a Never-Before-Seen Creature Biography, Shelter, and Timeline. At the end of the academic year, students placed their writings in sequence, and created a stand-alone book called, *The Adventures of Creatures in Cloud City*. My History Wall became a fundamental part of my teaching. Starting with empty walls, I added one of my Long-Range Planning Boards to the History Wall each month, along with student work. By the time my students completed all 10 of my Design Challenges (around June), my Long-Range Planning Boards were the centerpiece of the History Wall. This highly visible display of my strategic plan for the academic year informed and reassured my students, their parents, and my administrators that hands-on learning is serious learning."

The Committee Job Board on Joseph Lechner's History Wall displays the results of his Never-Before-Seen Leadership Design Challenge. It names the Mayor and City Council members of the student-built Cloud City, and lists committees with students' parallel roles in Cloud City and in the classroom. The Post-It Note colors identify each committee and area of responsibility. The Committee Job Board was accessible by students for daily use and revision as Joseph changed their committee jobs and leadership positions throughout the school year.

* * *

A comprehensive Design-Based Learning classroom is student-centered and encompasses these major academic goals of the K–12 curriculum: Knowledge, Critical and Creative Thinking, Cultural and Democratic Understanding (Civic Values), Skills Attainment, and Social Participation. Teachers are facilitators of a dual world: the student-built and student-governed City and the student-governed classroom. Students are taught how to communicate, collaborate, and self-advocate. Teachers share with students the Design Challenges and Guided Lessons that are in store for them during the school year and use the classroom walls as a display of the history of students' learning.

IN CLOSING

My mother was a strong and demanding force in our family. She always said that I did things backwards, calling me Moishe Kapoyr. That wasn't a compliment. In Yiddish, a Moishe Kapoyr always did everything the other way around: backwards.

Could that be why I developed a methodology that I call Backwards Thinking™?

She and my father, who had the spirit of an artist but was an unsuccessful entrepreneur with only a 4th-grade education, together raised two children who wanted to make a difference in the world.

Since the initial development of my methodology some 50 years ago at Westminster Elementary School in Venice, California, the Doreen Nelson Method of Design-Based Learning continues to be widely practiced in public and private schools at all grade levels and in all academic subjects.

Activating the spatial domain by having students roughly build and run a tabletop City, paired with my Backwards Thinking™ process for igniting creative thinking and integrating the curriculum, is proven to make learning stick. Even in the early development of my methodology, my students got better test scores when they no longer had to adhere to a rigid "frontward" learning process. Instead of feeling intimidated by test questions, they came to see themselves as courageous thinkers who could figure out answers.

The teachers I've been privileged to see embrace my methodology relate how students of all ages take ownership of everything that happens in "their" City as they shape it with their own hands, govern it through collaboration and decision-making, justify their inventions, delve into textbook studies, and revise their initial designs. It isn't surprising that students "get" how a City in the physical or virtual classroom promotes equity and social responsibility, and reflects their opinions, wishes, and dreams for a just future, giving purpose to their learning. It is teachers who make this possible. To me, they are society's true warriors.

ACKNOWLEDGMENTS

It takes a village and my village overflows with family, friends, and colleagues, eager to have my methodology honored and this book sent out into the world. I am grateful to them.

With her unwavering patience and belief in me, my editor, Lynne Heffley, guided the shaping of this book. I'm grateful to Barbara Isenberg for leading me to Lynne Heffley; to Mike Rose, who reminded me who the book was for, and to Paul Goldberger who encouraged me as a storyteller. Among others who generously contributed to the preparation of the manuscript, poring over the details, voicing their opinions, and giving loving, critical reviews: my former student, Jessica Heim; writer, editor, and gifted photographer Susan Morehead; my early reader, Phyllis Rosser; Charmaine Morano, always there for me in a pinch; my invaluable assistant, Nicolás Bejarano Isaza; and Erica Escobar, who has helped me for many years.

Thanks to photographer and long-time friend, Tom Vinetz, who jumped in at the last minute to review the photos; and to Scott Widmeyer, at Finn Partners, who guided and reassured me during the publication process, along with his team Marina Stenos and Kathleen Kennedy Manzo.

I am fortunate to have friends who have urged me to continue capturing my thinking about education in writing: Noma Copley, Flory Barnett, Sheila McCoy, Susan Morehead, Grace Arnold, Yasmin Kafai, John Iacovelli, Amanda Pope, Molly George, Robert Ramirez, my doctor, Lawrence Piro; and my therapists Peter Galvin and the late Miriam Williams.

In developing my methodology, I stood on the shoulders of a host of hero educators: John Dewey, who opened my eyes to how thinking about the meaning of teaching and learning can have a transformative effect on a teacher; Charlotte Crabtree, a professor of education at UCLA, who taught me how to organize Dewey's thinking into a course of study; Dewey's disciple, Corinne Seeds, who started the Lab School at UCLA where his pedagogy was practiced and where I was trained and taught; Hilda Taba, whose spiral curriculum illuminated for me the fact that a specific concept could be taught over and over, from kindergarten through high school, in different ways; Mee Lee Ling, my training teacher at the UCLA Lab School, and administrator Amber Wilson, both of whom understood my drive to bring to life the intellectual and philosophical underpinnings of classroom teaching and nurtured my determination to merge theory and practice; and Helen Heffernan, the Chief of the Bureau of Elementary Education for the State of California, who hired me as a demonstration teacher, watched me teach, and critiqued my lessons.

Thanks to my hero thinkers who influenced and contributed to my work over the years: psychologist and cognitive learning theorist Jerome Bruner, who became a friend and challenged me to prove that creativity could be taught; Benjamin Bloom, whose writing inspired me to put the teaching of higher-level thinking skills first; and educators, educational theorists, and philosophers Lev Vygotsky, Herbert Kohl, Ivan Illich, Paolo Freire, Maria Montessori, John McNeil, John Goodlad, and David Perkins.

I am grateful to so many who enabled me to extend and deepen the reach of my work: renowned designers Ray and Charles Eames championed National Endowment for the Arts funding for me to train teachers in my methodology, took thousands of photos of those classrooms, made slide shows, a film, and gave me office space and the resources to promote the work. Susan Hamilton, then-Director of the Smithsonian Institution Associates, oversaw the first intensive summer teacher-training program in my methodology at the Smithsonian for teachers from all over the country (and Ruth Heibert, from Sulphur Springs Union School District in California, was one exceptional teacher who picked up the baton and ran with it). Landscape architect Lawrence Halprin invited me to co-lead workshops with him, and aeronautical engineer and inventor Paul MacCready, who described my work at educational conferences as "pioneering the future," and funded the application of my methodology in a yearlong, middle school science program.

I am forever thankful to videographer Rachael Strickland for introducing me to computer scientist Alan Kay—and to Alan, who included me in his groundbreaking research for Apple Computer that Rachael was documenting at the L.A. Open Charter School, led by principal Bobby Blatt. As part of Alan's team, I was fortunate to collaborate with teachers Dolores Patton and Leslie Barclay in a yearlong application of my methodology in their joint classroom of 70 students; and with composer/bassoonist John Steinmetz to explore my methodology's aural applications. An unexpected bonus of my work with Alan Kay was getting to know mathematician/computer scientist Seymour Papert, a pioneer of artificial intelligence, who invited me to MIT as a scholar-in-residence; and Will Wright and Jeff Braun, who hired me to come play in their sandbox and write their teachers' guides as they refined the world of Sim City.

It is due to Sylvia Coop, the principal of Westminster Elementary School in Venice, California, who took a risk in the late 1960s and let me put my research into action in the classroom, that my methodology developed so quickly. By connecting me with veteran teacher Ruth Glatt, who worked tirelessly with me to turn my thinking into practice, Sylvia gave me the time and space to explore the intersection of creative thinking and required subject matter. (My friendship with Ruth has lasted through all the years since; Ruth ensured that I had a quiet place to begin writing this book, a house in Hawaii provided by her nephew, Jeffrey Milman.)

I doubt that I will ever find the right words to express my gratitude to that first class of 9- and 10-year-olds at Westminster, the students who became my coresearchers and critics: Jennifer Albert, Yolanda Benuelos, Diana Gardner, Adam Gardener, Elizabeth Gordon, Roger Grant, Portia Grimes, Terrance Hoke, Joseph Hopfield, Janet Jefferson, Jack Loera, Evelyn Lund, Tami Manzanaries, Randy Martin, Donna McLemore, Terry Meadows, Lisa Mendelsohn, Socorra Moldonado, Norma Proctor, Laura Robinson, Joseph Shea, John Shea, James Sherman, Brenda West, and Stephen Wilson. I've stayed in touch with many of them. Most recently, Portia Grimes spoke at a UCLA teacher-training event about the effect the methodology had on her life, and Donna McLemore tracked me down to tell me of her vivid memories of our time together.

My thanks go out to former USC architecture students Gilbert Stayner and Alan Gatzke (who had heard about my work and wanted to see what I was doing), photographer Teri Fox, USC professor Ralph Knowles, Elyse Grinstein and her family, and artist Ed Bereal, all of whom showed up regularly in my classroom to work with my students as they built the first-ever City and documented the process with Teri. With funding from the National Endowment for the Arts Architects-in-Schools Program, I was able to hire my brother, Frank, then a young architect, who taught with me and helped me select student architects Doug Moreland, Jaime Gesundheit, Richard Rowe, Jeff Vanderbort, Bob Simonian, Greg Spiess, Dan Benjamin, Ty Miller, and others to join me as I began training teachers throughout Greater Los Angeles. Through their commitment to my methodology, I developed a blueprint to enable K–12 teachers to use their skills to facilitate a student-built City in the classroom without a professional by their side.

I am profoundly grateful to those who saw to it that my work gained academic approval in college and university settings. The late Marvin Malecha, former Dean of the College of Environmental

Design at Cal Poly, Pomona, hired me in 1986 to develop a course of study based on my methodology, made sure that I was tenured after three years, and championed my work during my eight years of teaching there. Bob Suzuki, the university's President at the time, asked me to teach teachers my methodology in off-campus cohort groups of K–12 teachers, and assigned me to Sidney Ribeau, Vice President of Academic Affairs (later President of Howard University), who coached me in how to navigate the off-campus process and before leaving the university, assigned me to the School of Education and Integrated Studies. Interim Dean Sheila McCoy, an early supporter of my work, shepherded the establishment of a Master of Arts degree with an emphasis on Design-Based Learning (the first such degree in the nation) through the university's governing body, and continues to be a close friend and advisor, speaking with me nightly to get me to the finish line with this book. Dorothy MacNevin, Chair of the Education Department at Cal Poly, saw me through difficult times and taught me how to recruit teachers and guide them through the master's degree program.

It was my good fortune that Richard Koshalek, former President of ArtCenter College of Design in Pasadena, brought me there to start a program under David Walker, the Dean of Public Programs. Working with Paula Goodman, Director of K–12 Programs, we established the still-running ArtsCenter for Kids program, the Design-Based Learning Summer Institute for K–12 Teachers, and informational workshops for school administrators. The Summer Institute thrived for nearly 20 years, thanks to the direct involvement and continuous support of Lorne Buchman, Richard's successor.

Unexpectedly, my retirement from Cal Poly in 2018 led to the forging of a relationship with UCLA School of Education and Information Studies. I felt that I had come home, because I was a graduate of UCLA, had taught in the UCLA Lab School, and was honored in 2017 as the first educator whose work was exhibited in the university's Charles E. Young Research Library, Special Collections, thanks to Marcia Melkonian, Curator/Manuscripts Librarian Genie Guerard; and Project Archivist Kelly Besser, who organized my work with deep understanding and recorded my oral history. The three-month exhibition led to a new platform for my work and I am grateful to Marcelo Suárez-Orozco (then Dean of the Graduate School of Education and Information Studies, now Chancellor of the University of Massachusetts, Boston), Christina "Tina" Christie (Marcello's successor), Professor Megan Franke, Center X Executive Director Annamarie Francois, and Senior Director of Development Amy Lassere, who positioned my methodology as part of UCLA's teacher-training.

A big thanks to other individuals and organizations that have underscored the boundless applications of my methodology. Singer/composer and treasured friend Anna Pangalou taught classes in my methodology and incorporated it into her music teaching practice in Greece. Architects Shinya Sato, Hiroko Hosoda, and others in Japan, through a cultural exchange program, brought my work into classrooms and showcased it in an exhibition at the Sendai Science Museum. Gordon Davidson, Founding Artistic Director of Center Theatre Group in Los Angeles, provided matching funds for a three-year NEA grant to apply my methodology to the teaching of underserved kids about theater. At the Lotus Music and Dance School in New York, my program called Dancing Across Cultural Borders featured dance forms from around the globe, and was taught in New York public schools. The methodology was studied at England's Royal College of Art during my one-year NEA fellowship as visiting scholar. It was applied by the American Bar Association to its Law-Related Education Program, and to the development of a Career Education Project for three California State University campuses and science programs at the Cabrillo Marine Aquarium in San Pedro, the Aquarium of the Pacific in Long Beach, and the Weizmann Institute in Israel, where I was scholar-in-residence.

A methodology is only as good as the teachers who make something out of it. The teachers whose classroom practice I describe in the book are among the many who have made my methodology their own. It has been my privilege to call them my colleagues. I am exceptionally proud of those teachers in the master's program at Cal Poly who developed their own programs using my methodology, opened their classrooms as demonstration sites, and became teacher-trainers themselves (many hired by Cal Poly to teach in the master's program; some hired as faculty to teach the methodology at ArtCenter in Pasadena and at UCLA Center X): Natalie Bezdjian, Kate Borihane, Nancy Buck, Terry Ceja, Daphne Chase, Miguel Fernandez, Araceli Garcia, Jessica Heim, Don Huey (the very first graduate in the master's program), Stephanie Na, Leakana Nhem, Richard Rosa, Cynthia Sicairos, Jennifer Sorbara, Leslie Stoltz, Temi Taylor (who applied my methodology to teach high school chemistry, the first time I found the subject understandable), and Emily Tilton, among others.

I owe special thanks to those teachers who have expanded the application of the methodology and given it prominence in unexpected ways. When Jessica Heim came to study with me in the master's program, her determination to learn the methodology was extraordinary. At the time, she was a full-time elementary school teacher, her son was a newborn, her daughter was six, and her father was terminally ill, yet Jessica not only got her degree and became a magnificent practitioner of my methodology, she began training other teachers. Luckily, she was willing to leave her stellar 15 years of classroom teaching in 2019 to take on the immense leadership role of Director, Design-Based Learning, UCLA Center X. Two years on, under Jessica's guidance, the program is blossoming. Leslie Stoltz, an early graduate of the master's program, was a marvelous overachiever, embracing the methodology and going on to develop a 6th-, 7th-, and 8th-grade program at her school in the Walnut Valley Unified School District, teach teachers at Cal Poly, travel with me to Japan to establish and run the exchange program, write teacher guides and syllabi with me, and become the principal of a charter school with Design-Based Learning as its mission. Leslie, who died in 2010, personified the very meaning of a gifted educator. A Design-Based Learning building on her middle school campus was named in Leslie's honor to showcase the work she began. Math teacher Jennifer Sorbara, Leslie's former teaching partner at the middle school, sculpted the methodology into the outstanding Academic Design Program at Walnut High School. She worked with teachers from varied subject areas to develop and sustain this three-year, interdisciplinary, immersive program for students who apply to take part (students like Madeleine Skinner, who refers to the program as a transformative experience and who is now training to become a teacher herself). Jennifer, an inspirational teacher of teachers, doesn't hesitate to question me as we plan teacher-training courses together, and I love it. I am indebted to Daphne Chase, who wrote to President Obama's Secretary of Education in 2016, relating how my methodology dovetailed with the Administration's belief in the importance of makers, builders, and doers to meet the nation's challenges, and who conveyed the significance of the methodology to administrators and teachers throughout the goes out San Gabriel Unified School District, leading to ongoing, in-depth teacher trainings in that district.

My gratitude to administrators in a variety of school districts: Los Angeles Unified School District, where I started teaching in 1959; Eugene Tucker, who has supported my work throughout his years as a superintendent of schools, beginning in the Sulphur Springs Union School District and the multi-city ABC Unified School District, and as faculty at UCLA, and whose guidance was invaluable in bringing my methodology to the UCLA School of Education; Ron Hockwell, who oversaw the development of the work Leslie Stolz began; Pomona Unified School District, Hacienda-La Puente Unified School District, Pasadena Unified School District, El Monte City School District,and Rowland Unified School District, among others. My eternal admiration goes to Superintendent Jim Symonds for his consistent and methodical guidance in expanding the work that Daphne Chase started in the San Gabriel Unified School District. Other exceptionally supportive administrators who made a difference: Angie De Martinez, Emma Hullett, Grace Arnold, Jeff Seymour, and Georgia Lazo.

Thanks to the truly extraordinary people, who through their wise counsel and unstinting financial and moral support, have kept the lights on for my nonprofit, The Center for City Building Education, started in 1974, giving me the freedom to take advantage of every opportunity to maintain the immediacy of my work and to continually adapt its applications in multiple settings. Among them, my Center for City Building Education Board members—Vice President Alan Mandell, who not only gives regular financial support, but who has listened tirelessly to my woes for over 40 years; Secretary Bobbi Mapstone, who as my confidant and invaluable assistant, despite having no formal teaching background, successfully took over my teacher-training during the year that I was bedridden with an injury; Treasurer Marcia Melkonian, who assisted me in countless ways for 30 years, making me an honorary member of her family as her daughter, Dvin, and son, Arin, came along to help; and my nephew, artist Alejandro Gehry, a recent addition to our Board, who has already made an impact with his commitment and expertise. Among our valued advisors: famed scientist Jonas Salk, Gloria Steinem, Gordon Davidson, Susan Hamilton, Lawrence Halprin, Nicholas England, Mel Powell, Morton Subotnick, John Goodlad, John Steinmetz, John Iacovelli, Hiroko

Hosoda, and Lev Gonick. My endless gratitude to them and to so many others whose generosity has enabled the work to flourish: Nicholas Beck, who named the Center in his will with a sizeable donation; my closest friends, musician Thomas Buckner and dancer Kamala Cesar Buckner, who have provided sustained financial support since 1991; and Andy Florian, my former driver, who gives a monthly donation out of his Netflix salary. Major donor Thomas L. Safran, along with Susan and Jaime Gesundheit, Susan Morehead, and Abby Sher, made the launch of the Design-Based Learning Project at UCLA Center X possible. A Thomas L. Safran Scholarship Fund provides for teachers in underserved communities to be trained at UCLA in the methodology; and the Frank O. Gehry Foundation has ensured the future of the methodology with a multimillion-dollar gift establishing the Doreen Gehry Nelson Director of Design-Based Learning endowed position at UCLA Center X.

Thank you, too, to the amazing teachers who have become Fellows of The Center for City Building Education: Jennifer Sorbara, Kate Borihane, Daphne Chase, Rana Masri, Yvette Villaseñor, David Cameron, Georgia Singleton, Araceli Garcia, Stephanie Na, Natalie Bezdjian, and Emily Tilton.

In my work and in my life, I am indebted to those who defy tradition and make things better by bringing their ideas into being. The classics have informed my life, but it is the artists, musicians, dancers, architects, writers, and furniture and clothing designers who break the boundaries of the old that I look to for inspiration. Seeing or hearing their works sets me on fire. These are some of the artists who played a big part in giving me permission to think differently: Joanna Beal, Cliff H. C. "Cliff" Westermann, Jess Collins, Ken Price, John Altoon, John Chamberlain, Edward Keinholz, Irving Petlin, Joe Goode, Yvonne de Miranda, Judy Baca, Wallace Berman, Lucas Samaras, Gwynn Murrill, Robert Indiana, Frank Stella, Louise Nevelson, and Mark Rothko.

The Surrealists—Renee Magritte, Max Ernst, Marcel Duchamp—resonated strongly with my conviction that renaming ordinary things sparks original thinking. Claes Oldenburg, who changed the size and scale of everyday objects, and Joseph Cornell, who turned boxes into worlds, fueled my use of scale and miniaturization in my work. As I was refining my methodology, I was influenced by artists whose work I began collecting: Robyn Denny, Carol Furr, Leo Robinson, Alexis Smith, and fashion designer Issey Miyake. After training as a classical harpist, I was inspired by the originality of cutting edge composers like John Cage, Harry Partch, La Monte Young (a fellow student at UCLA, who wrote a solo harp piece for me to perform), and Anne LeBaron, who honored me with a performance of her composition, "Poem for Doreen."

Finally, I am beyond grateful for the love of my family. My big brother, mentor, and friend, the tradition-defying, boundary-breaking, architect extraordinaire Frank Gehry, taught with me, gave me space in his office in the 1970s as I began spreading my methodology, has always egged me on to do more, took the time to read the draft of this book, and is determined to see that the word gets out—and his wife Berta, sister, confidant, and dearest friend, who has been there for me, step by step. Together, Frank and Berta, through their love and the Gehry Foundation, have provided for the continuation of my work in perpetuity. Our parents would be proud of all that we have both accomplished. I am, too.

INDEX